RENEWING REFORMED THEOLOGY

A UNITED REFORMED CHURCH PUBLICATION

A collection of papers given at
a conference in Autumn 2010 at
Westminster College, Cambridge

The
United
Reformed
Church

granary
A URC PUBLICATION

First published in Great Britain in 2012 by the United Reformed Church,
86 Tavistock Place, London WC1H 9RT

www.urc.org.uk

A CIP catalogue record for this book
Is available from the British Library.

ISBN: 978-0-85346-290-3

Contents

A set of essays exploring the theme of reformed theology and where it might take us.

Renewing Reformed Theology

RENEWING REFORMED THEOLOGY
A clear identity...

Martin Camroux

"Nondescript Christianity, featureless Christianity, is a little bit too close to the truth for comfort. We need to be clear — a robust sense of ecclesial identity is healthy for a church."

A clear identity...

Martin Camroux

How strong is the United Reformed Church's (URC's) identity as a Church and how much is that shaped by our Reformed Theology? Some years in search of pastures new I went to meet the Elders at a URC in a sumptuous Thameside London suburb. The following conversation took place.

Q. What is the theological position of this church?
A. Can you repeat the question?

Q. What is the theological position of this church?
A. Can you explain the question?

Q. What is this church doing locally for unity?
A. That's a good question.

Q. Do you support Commitment for Life?
A. What is Commitment for Life?

Q. Why should anyone come to this church and not to the thriving Baptist Church around the corner?

A. Because they're Scots.

I made none of that up. Is this typical of the United Reformed Church? I do hope not. Is it symptomatic of the state of the church? I cannot entirely deny it with the vigour I would wish to!

The Church Life Survey of 2001 found only 25% of URC members had a strong commitment to the Church. Of all denominations URC members moving to another area are least likely to maintain their denominational link. Very few church members if asked what the Reformed tradition is can give a coherent answer.

If the URC lacks identity and definition there are a variety of possible causes. In part it is a by-product of the URC's ecumenical commitment. Before it was established the URC gave very little thought as to its Reformed identity. Its hope was that its creation would break the ecumenical log-jam. What needs to define the ethos of the URC if the church was simply a staging post on a journey – which is another way of saying that beyond its ecumenical commitment the church's founders had little vision of its nature or role.

When the early hopes of union proved illusory the question of what the United Reformed Church's distinguishing characteristics were was fundamental but instinctively it seemed unecumenical to explore it. For many years there was an almost total lack of serious ecclesiology. It was not until 1998, and the publication of David Cornick's *Under God's Good Hand* that a history of the traditions which came together in the United Reformed Church was published. Today it is no longer in print. It was 2002 (thirty years after the church's foundation!) before the United Reformed Church published David Peel's *Reforming Theology* which set out to explore the theological ethos of the United Reformed Church.

> Before it was established the URC gave very little thought as to its Reformed identity. Its hope was that its creation would break the ecumenical log-jam.

In reality creating a United Reformed out of Congregationalists and Presbyterians was always a more difficult problem than most people realised. This was not simply a union of two very similar Reformed Churches. Congregationalism was never a classical Reformed church but a blend of Reformed and radical Anabaptist. As Forsyth points out, if Calvinism was the father of Independency, Anabaptist theology was its mother. History deepened the divide. In the 18th and 19th centuries

Congregationalism was renewed first by the Evangelical Revival and then by liberalism. Calvinism was abandoned and almost forgotten. As David Cornick has reminded us Charles Silvester Horne could write a history of the Free Churches with only one reference to Calvin – that his influence had hindered the development of church music![1]

So when you create the URC what do you have? You have a Church where most people have never seen themselves as Reformed and denominational leaders who feel the need to down play their heritage partly for ecumenical reasons and partly because their life's work has been to edge away from the traditions of independency in order to create a United Reformed Church.

Put this Church in the individualistic consumer culture of late modernity where all religious identities are eroded and it's hardly surprising if you end up with a Church with an identity problem. A few wise souls saw this coming. Let me at this point pay a tribute to Arthur Macarthur, who died two years ago, and had a sharper mind than almost anyone involved in the creation of the URC. At the time of the earlier talks between Presbyterians and Anglicans Arthur Macarthur warned that losing touch with the Anglicans would mean that "any union between the Congregational Church and ourselves would result in a united church confused about its purpose and unable to find a role". Writing in 1997 he said, "I sometimes feel the chill of that prophecy."[2]

At this point we have to ask ourselves some fundamental questions about our ecumenical theology. Importantly we need to see that diversity is as much God given as unity. At Iona they use the call to worship:

How good and lovely it is
to live together in unity.

Ian Bradley says, that when they do say this, he substitutes the word diversity for unity:

> How good and lovely it is
> **to live together in diversity.**

That is equally true. If it is we do not forward real ecumenism by homogenizing theological traditions.

Karl Barth is worth listening to here. Barth is explicit about the scandal of Christian disunity. "There is no justification" he wrote "theological, spiritual or biblical, for the existence of a plurality of churches genuinely separated – and mutually excluding each other. A plurality of churches in this sense means a plurality of lords... a plurality of gods".[3] He goes on, however, to argue that the way to unity is not by churches ceasing to take their distinctiveness seriously, "by denying and renouncing their special character for the sake of internal or external peace, by trying to exist in a kind of nondescript Christianity" – a state of ecclesiological "featurelessness".[4] In fact the continued existence of separate churches can only be justified when they claim to represent something vital for faith and salvation[5]

That is a warning that we in the URC need to hear. Nondescript Christianity, featureless Christianity, is a little bit too close to the truth for comfort. We need to be clear – a robust sense of ecclesial identity is healthy for a church. Indeed if we do not believe our tradition has something of fundamental value there cannot be any justification for our continuing as a separate denomination.

I am arguing that re-engaging with Reformed theology is a vital necessity not only for the vitality of our Church but for our ecumenical commitment too. This is a demanding task. As T.S. Eliot once said, "Tradition is not something you inherit. If you want it you must obtain it with great labour. You've got to fight for it. You don't gain access to traditions by means of osmosis."[6] If we want a blessing, like Jacob we shall have to wrestle for it.

The Reformed tradition is not a list of theological propositions. It is a living tradition, one which – as John

Buchanan says it – "resists being pinned down too precisely, instead preserves its own energy and responsibility to respond to history, which is constantly changing".

In origin, as Philip Benedict shows, the Reformed tradition was always "multi-vocal" Calvin is certainly the most forceful voice but the Reformed Churches were independent and maintained their own particular emphases. "The leading Reformed theologians of this period were all independent thinkers who did not see eye to eye on every point of doctrine, while the churches that became the source and model for the Reformed tradition's expansion differed from each other in crucial organizational details."[7] One of the features that Bruce Gordon brings out well in his recent biography of Calvin is the way he engages in debate with other Reformed leaders and is often willing to modify his positions to reach agreement. So he debates with Bullinger over predestination, with Bucer who was something of a father figure to him, and with Melanchthon and the Lutherans over the Eucharist. He never attempted to impose his views on church organization on others and did not think that Geneva was the only model. As Gordon puts it, "As long as God's commandments are obeyed and Christians live together in love the external forms of community can vary according to necessity."[8]

> "As long as God's commandments are obeyed and Christians live together in love the external forms of community can vary according to necessity."

As the Reformed family spreads so does the diversity. One of the values of Diarmaid MacCulloch's wonderful biography of Cranmer is the extent to which he shows Cranmer to be a Reformed theologian, close in view to Bucer, but willing to accept episcopacy[9]. With Congregationalism, the debate goes wider. Congregationalism adopts a view of the local congregation which had led Calvin to excommunicate

Morely and publicly burn his Treatise in Geneva, despite being godfather to one of his children. It developed a commitment to religious toleration very distinct from Calvin. When you come across the words, "I had rather that Mohammedanism be permitted amongst us, than that one of God's children should be persecuted" you will be likely to mistakenly attribute this to Calvin. When the Genevan state burnt the Unitarian Michael Servetus, Calvin's hatred of him was clear, though he did advocate beheading as more merciful. Compare that with Cromwell's reaction to the very similar views of John Biddle where Cromwell intervened to ensure that Biddle was not executed, but instead sent to exile on the Isles of Scilly. The glory of this tradition is John Milton's *Areopagitica*. "No man, no synod, no session of men, though called the church, can judge definitely the sense of Scripture to another man's conscience."

> The principle of *Sola Scriptura* and Calvin's tendency to equate faith with assenting to doctrinal propositions led directly to literalism and fundamentalism.

The Reformed tradition is not a simple set of propositions. In fact quite diverse, and even incompatible, theologies find an origin in it. Both fundamentalism and liberalism have roots in the Reformation. The principle of *Sola Scriptura* and Calvin's tendency to equate faith with assenting to doctrinal propositions led directly to literalism and fundamentalism. Yet the emphasis on close examination of the text of scripture, together with a commitment to toleration and liberty of conscience, led to the Enlightenment and to liberalism, with thinkers such as John Milton and John Locke. Today in the URC both *Free to Believe* and *GEAR* can claim Reformed ancestry.

Re-engaging with Reformed theology therefore is not a simple process like taking an oven ready dinner and warming it up. It can come only to a limited extent from Church counsels and committees. It must primarily come from theologians and preachers and congregations wresting with the gospel's meaning and our contemporary life in such a way as can give us hope. We must wrestle for a blessing.

> On a huge hill,
> Cragged and steep, Truth stands, and he that will
> Reach her, about must and about must go,
> And what the hill's suddenness resists, win so.[10]

To succeed in this, as Canada's Douglas John Hall, puts it, "Our churches do not need managers, they need thinkers! They need people whose knowledge of the Scriptures, traditions, and contemporary Christian scholarship is *more developed* than has been required of clergy in the past."[11]

We should not expect just one vision to come out of this. The diversity of the tradition and individual conviction will inevitably lead to diversity of interpretation. But for the Reformed Christian theological debate is part of the living heart of the Church and ought to be welcomed as part of our renewal. Debate, argument, inspiration go together.

Does it matter whether we succeed or not in reconnecting with our tradition? I think so. Today the Church needs all the vitality it can get. So let me give 6 features which excite me.

ONE

Firstly it excites me to be part of a tradition that sees everything as open to challenge and change. I am excited by the great Reformation slogan. *Ecclesia Reformata, Semper Reformanda*: **The church reformed and always to be reformed.** There is at the heart of our tradition, a commitment to self-examination and self-criticism, a willingness to recognise that theology and institutional structures are no more than provisional, and always open to change in the face of new challenges and new light from God. This is what Paul Tillich called that "Protestant principle," God alone is ultimate—everything else is open to Reformation.

I grew up loving George Rawson's hymn

"We limit not the truth of God
To our poor reach of mind
By notions of our day and sect
Crude partial and confined."[12]

Which of course bring us to the words of Pastor John Robinson: "That the Lord hath yet more light and truth to break forth from his word".

I was so proud to be part of a church that sang that. And I am proud to be part of a church in whose Basis of Union we read, "The United Reformed Church...acknowledges its duty to be open at all times to the leading of the Holy Spirit and therefore affirms its right to make such new declarations of faith...as may from time to time be required by obedience to that same Spirit". If I may borrow from the other side of the Atlantic we believe that God is still speaking, that we should "Never place a period where God has placed a comma."

TWO

Reformed Theology is biblical theology. The Reformation brings a new kind of Christianity because, with the invention of the printing press, it is now possible to have widespread personal access to the scriptures. For Calvin the Scriptures are to be regarded as having "Sprung from heaven" and the medium through which "the living words of God are heard."[13] If there is new light and truth it is from the Word it comes. There is a fundamental logic to this. The Bible is not simply the sole historical source for the events upon which our faith is based; it is also the primary source of reflection upon those events. It is therefore indispensable for faith. Professor Howard Marshall puts it better than I ever could: "It is through the Bible that I know of the God who has declared his salvation in the life, death and resurrection of Jesus, and with deepest thankfulness I embrace that saving truth and stake my life on it". It excites me to be part of a tradition whose deepest impulse is to open the book.

We cannot however leave the matter here. The centrality of Scripture was to prove more problematic than the Reformers imagined. *Sola Scriptura* (by scripture alone) is a dangerous concept. It might mean that all that was necessary for a saving faith could be found in scripture, but it could be, and often was, taken to mean that the gospel comes only from scripture and that there is no need to contextualize it in contemporary knowledge or culture. Calvin sometimes seems to encourage such an understanding, "The apostles were only the sworn notaries of the Holy Spirit, so that their Scriptures might be held authentic: the successors have no other commission than to teach what they find contained in the Holy Scriptures."[14]

In the light of this it is unsurprising that Reformed theology was to be a major source of biblical fundamentalism and ironically encouraged a denial of serious study of the Scriptures and an unreflective sanctifying of individual prejudice with the authority of God. Such fundamentalism has been a primary source of conflict with science, has often led to contempt of historical study, and been the source of opposition to many social reforms. By encouraging people to believe they know the whole truth fundamentalism poisons religion. As Rabbi Tony Bayfield, the head of Reform Judaism, put it, "It is not only arrogance to the point of madness but potentially bad to the point of evil".

> By encouraging people to believe they know the whole truth fundamentalism poisons religion.

Fundamentalism is a danger to evangelical religion. It forgets that in its primary sense the word of God is not the Bible – but Christ. It's task is to witness to him, not to itself. As Coffin perceptively puts it, "When I was in seminary, Richard Niebuhr taught that the Bible is "an indispensable means seeking its dispensability.' In other words, it is a signpost not a hitching post. It points beyond itself, saying, 'Pay attention to God, not me.'"[15]

None of this takes away from my love as a Reformed Christian of the Bible. In fact the Reformed tradition contains correctives which enable me to hold together a love of the Scriptures with a love of the reasoned word in such a way that both are enhanced. No-one who really values the reasoned word will make the mistake of imaging that there is no worthwhile knowledge outside scripture – anymore than Calvin did. For Calvin the most important source of truth was scripture. But second to that came philosophy. In every age, he said philosophers have been stimulated by God "that they might enlighten the world in knowledge of the truth". In the very opening word of the Institutes of the Christian religion he draws on Cicero's definition of philosophy. What is more it is the Calvin who

> Ours is a tradition which gives a central place to serious theology, serious thinking, and serious preaching.

champions *Sola Scriptura* who says "We are at liberty to borrow from any source anything that has come from God".[16] As Coffin says, "Christians have to listen to the world as well as to the word – to science, to history, to what our reason and experience tell us. We do not honour the higher truth we find in Christ by ignoring truths found elsewhere"[17] If you look over the west portal of Harry Emerson Fosdick's Riverside Church in New York, where Coffin ministered, you will find a range of sculptures. Here is Mohammed, Buddha and Confucius. Also here is a group of scientists including Charles Darwin and Albert Einstein. Nothing could more explicitly affirm the proper Reformed openess to diverse sources of truth.

THREE

Ours is a tradition which gives a central place to serious theology, serious thinking, and serious preaching. In the **New York Times'** Peter Steinfels says that Calvin, "did as much as anyone to shape the modern world: his legacy has been traced to everything from modern marriage and modern science to modern liberal government and modern capitalism." How did he do that? From his study and the pulpit. What made him the most important figure of the Reformation – the quality of his ideas! Calvin was simply one of the most brilliant, if not the most brilliant, intellects of his age. Bruce Gordon says of him, "Calvin felt as if he had never met his intellectual equal and he was probably right."[18] Calvin motivated Protestantism by giving it a powerful, coherent, challenging theology; above all he produced *The Institutes of the Christian Religion* – one of the great intellectual achievements in Christian history.

Today Christianity has been relegated to the sidelines of our culture. Sometimes we collude in this ourselves. I heard Brian Wren the other day telling of a worship service with overhead projector. One of the hymns went something like. *Jesus, Jesus, Jesus. Jesus Jesus Jesus. Jesus Jesus Jesus.* And then at the bottom it said *repeat three times*.

The URC is a church with no serious theological journal, diminishing theological resources in its colleges, and few serious academic theologians, even fewer of whom are actually employed by the denomination. Today, as the Pope has reminded us, we face a Europe which has largely forgotten what faith means. But if we're going to offer a gospel that can change this we need to remember what Jack Spong meant when he said, "The heart cannot worship what the mind has rejected". We need to connect people with questions to a God they can believe in. And that requires serious theology, serious thinking, and serious preaching. What was it Calvin said; the elect obey the voice of reason.

FOUR

The Reformed tradition is political. Luther was willing to draw a line between religion and politics. "There is the kingdom of God," he said, "and there is the kingdom of this world – and as for the kingdom of this world let him take it who will". For Calvin however, a central belief of Christians was the sovereignty of God and therefore God's will included politics. Calvin believed that it was the role of religion to move out of the church and into the world:

that the content of the church's creeds and confession must be expressed not only liturgically but socially and politically and economically. Wealth for example was given by God to meet the needs of the community, especially those in need. "The hungry are defrauded of their rights if their hunger is not relieved." So the community must provide practical provision for the poor.

Today this is visibly demonstrated in the United Reformed Church's contribution to Church and Society, Commitment for Life, Jubilee debt campaign, Make Poverty History and its opposition to the illegal, immoral and foolish Iraq war. I sometimes hear it said that this is simply a reflection of the fact that the United Reformed Church contains quite a few Guardian readers. That undervalues it. The Reformed tradition has always been political because it knows that, as Bill Coffin used to say, "The prophet did not say "Let charity flow down like mighty waters" ... The prophet said "Let justice flow down like waters, and *righteousness like an overflowing stream".[19]* That is in our Reformed DNA! As Andrew Marvell put it, the task of Reformed religion is

> "to cast the kingdoms old
> Into another mould"[20]

FIVE

From the Reformed tradition came a new idea of the Church – with authority coming from the bottom not the top and with people having the right to elect their leaders both in church and state. Calvin himself had an authoritarian streak. When Pierre Ameaux challenged his teaching on predestination he was forced to walk through the city dressed only in a shirt and carrying a torch. While supporting the free election of Church officers he regarded democracy as "the most troublesome and most seditious form of Church government" It left doctrinal and disciplinary decisions to the "whim" of the congregation. Anyone who has ever been to General Assembly will not be unsympathetic to that. But look at the First Book of Discipline of the Church of Scotland,

- Ministers to be elected by their congregations.
- Elders to be elected annually
- Everyone from the highest to the lowest to be subject to spiritual discipline.
- A system of poor relief to be introduced and a school in every parish.[21]

Now you've started something. Once you elect officers in Church then why not in the state too? Listen to Andrew Melville telling King James, 'God's silly vassal', there are two kingdoms in Scotland. First and foremost there is the kingdom of Christ, in which James is not a king nor the head, but the mere member. No wonder when he had the chance James put him in the tower of London. Said James: "If you aim at a Scots presbytery, it agreeth as well with monarchie as God and the devil."[22]

Our task is to be a distinctively non-hierarchical church, which understands that once you have knelt by someone at the Eucharist you cannot claim social superiority in the world, that indeed that, *"the poorest he that is in England hath a life to live, as the greatest he"* (Rainsborough.)

SIX
I am excited by a religious tradition that so unambiguously proclaims the graciousness of God. Reformed theology is a theology of grace, resting on Paul's understanding of faith and salvation as God's gifts in Jesus Christ. We cannot win or earn our salvation. It is given in Jesus Christ. We cannot secure it by works of the law, by religious ritual, by following religion or church requirements. The Reformed tradition is of a God of unimaginable grace.

We cannot secure (salvation) by works of the law, by religious ritual, by following religion or church requirements.

The other week I was at a service where we were asked to sing, "My only desire is to be holy". Would it were true! The reality is quite otherwise.

Just as I thou tossed about
with many a conflict many a doubt,
fightings and fears within, without,
O Lamb of God I come.[23]

The Gospel is of God of grace, who accepts us not because of what we are but out of love. The Church above all must sound the note of grace, a grace that excludes no-one.

A Reformed identity is not of itself sufficient to attract consumers in the spiritual cafeteria of modern day religion. If it was the Church of Scotland would not be in such calamitous decline. But in a post-Christian age local churches which are going to thrive need a motivating theology which can both give a powerful purpose for their existence and offer a powerful version of the Christian gospel.

There's a nice story told about Heinrich Heine, the German, or if you prefer Jewish, poet, which Bill Coffin used to tell. Heine was standing with a friend before the great cathedral of Amiens in France. The friend said "Heinrich, tell me why people can't build piles like this anymore? And Heine answers, "Cher ami, it's really very easy. In those days people had convictions, we modern have opinions and it takes more than an opinion to build a cathedral".

It takes more than opinions to build a church. One 17th century observer said: "I had rather see coming toward me a whole regiment with drawn swords, than one lone Calvinist convinced that he is doing the will of God." Reformed theology is a living tradition which commits us not to a static set of beliefs but to a renewed search for a dynamic and self-critical theology. Renewal will come from theologically active local congregations with a vision of what the gospel is and a delight in it.

Ecclesia Reformata, Semper Reformanda: **The church reformed and always to be reformed.**

References

[1] Charles Silvester Horne, *A Popular History of the Free Churches*, James Clarke. London1903, p249

[2] Arthur Macarthur, *"Setting Up Signs,"* United Reformed Church, London, 1997, p 89

[3] Karl Barth, *Church Dogmatics*, G.W. Bromley and T.F. Torrance (eds), Edinburgh, T A T Clark, 1975 p 675

[4] Ibid p 678

[5] Ibid p 680

[6] T. S Eliot, *Tradition and Individual Talent*, 1919

[7] Philip Benedict *Christ's Churches Purely Reformed*, New Haven, Yale University Press, 2002, p 55

[8] Bruce Gordon, *Calvin*, New Haven, Yale university Press, 2009 p 276

[9] Diarmaid MacCulloch, *Thomas Cranmer*, New Haven, Yale University Press, 1996

[10] John Donne Satire 111

[11] Douglas John Hall, *Professing the Faith*, (Minneapolis: Fortress Press, 1998), p195

[12] Congregational Praise No 230

[13] Calvin, *Institutes, 1,6,1*

[14] Calvin, Institutes, iv,8,9

[15] William Sloane Coffin, *The Heart is a Little to the Left*, University Press of New England, Hanover, 1999. p 49

[16] Comm. I Cor 15.33 citing Paul's example: Comm Titus 1:12, citing Basil.

[17] Coffin op.cit p 49

[18] Bruce Gordon, Calvin, Yale University Press, New Haven, 2009, p vii

[19] William Sloane Coffin *Credo*, Westminster John Know Press, Louisville, 2004, 65

[20] Andrew Marvell, *Poems*, London, `Heinemann, 1969, p 119

[21] Harry Reid, *Reformation,* Saint Andrew Press, Edinburgh, 2010, p 244-5

[22] Adam Nicolson, God Secretaries: The Making of the King James Bible, Harper Collins, New York, 2004, p 56

[23] Charlotte Elliott, *Congregational Praise*, No. 385

A UNITED REFORMED CHURCH PUBLICATION

RENEWING REFORMED THEOLOGY
The Reformed and ecumenism

David Cornick

"Despite the present troubles of the
Anglican Communion, Anglicans and
Lutherans have a more strongly
developed sense of communion than the
Reformed. So, what is it in Reformed
DNA than makes it particularly prone
to division?"

The
United
Reformed
Church

The Reformed and ecumenism...

David Cornick

I n 1552 John Calvin famously responded warmly to Archbishop Thomas Cranmer's suggestion of a general meeting of Europe's Protestants. ' ...the churches are so divided, that human fellowship is scarcely now in any repute amongst us, far less that Christian intercourse which all make a profession of, but few sincerely practise...Thus is it that the members of the Church being severed, the body lies bleeding. So much does this concern me, that, if I could be of any service, I would not grudge to cross even ten seas, if need be, on account of it.'[1] It never happened because Edward VI was dead within a year and Cranmer speeding his way to a martyr's death. Nine years later Calvin mooted the idea to Matthew Parker, Elizabeth's Archbishop. He expressed interest, but nothing happened.

During the summer of 2010, at Grand Rapids in Michigan, the World Communion of Reformed Churches was born from the union of the World Alliance of Reformed Churches and the Reformed Ecumenical Council – 80 million believers in 230 denominations in over 100 countries. Whilst it is encouraging that the Reformed have at last felt able to form a communion, the statistics give ample evidence of an embarrassing reality of Reformed life. Reformed churches splinter like glass, and have scant regard for their own internal unity. They have split over serious doctrinal questions, church government, relations to the state, oaths, and even restoring the unity of the church.

It is, of course, a mistake to regard the Reformed tradition as Calvinist. It was piebald at its birth, rooted in the differing reformations of the cities and cantons of Switzerland. However, it would be equally mistaken to believe that Calvinism became anything other than the dominating theological system within the tradition. The paradox that the tradition which revered an apostle of unity became one of the greatest sources of division in church history merits investigation.

Of Calvin's devotion to unity there is little doubt. Calvin was eight when Luther nailed his theses to the church door in Wittenberg, and by the time he emerged onto the Genevan stage as a serious player, the reformations had been underway for twenty years. He was powerless to prevent its splintering – that had already happened. Nonetheless, he took part in a handful of Protestant-Catholic colloquies in his youth, even though it was unlikely that they would achieve anything.[2] To his dying day he longed for a more ecumenical council than Trent (1546). Lukas Vischer described Calvin's concern for the unity of Protestantism as a 'red thread' running through his ministry.[3] His *Short Treatise on the Lord's Supper* (1540) still stands as an outstanding model of ecumenical theology as he sought agreement between Lutheran and Zwinglian eucharistic theologies.[4] It didn't work, but he tried. The spirit of Bucer, that more eirenic of reformers, with whom he had ministered in Strasbourg, burnt within him. However, he was successful in creating an agreement between the German speaking Swiss of Zurich and Francophone Geneva – the *Concensus Tigurinus* of 1549 which he and Bullinger drew up was, as Alec Ryrie has recently noted '...the most genuinely successful interconfessional agreement of the sixteenth century.'[5]

> Whilst it is encouraging that the Reformed have at last felt able to form a communion, the statistics give ample evidence of an embarrassing reality of Reformed life.

Of Calvin's commitment to the unity of Protestantism there can be no doubt. Granted it didn't reach as far as the Anabaptists, but at least he didn't drown them as Zwingli did. Calvin's world was very different to ours. His concern was for recognition of confessions, for co-operation wherever possible between Lutherans, the Church of England and the Protestant churches of Europe. But it is worth noting that his concern is with visible, real historical communities, and in that sense his concern for unity bears similarities to contemporary ecumenical endeavour.

The Reformed were, from the beginning, convinced catholics, deeply conscious that they were seeking to restore the true church, to re-form it. Their best works are drenched in the early church fathers. Bullinger prefaces his *Decades* with eleven creeds of the early church, and affirmed the first four ecumenical councils. In the fifty sermons that make up the book he is at pains to demonstrate that he believes this to be the faith of the Holy Catholic Church, and that the church of Zurich is in continuity with it.[6] Calvin himself has long been regarded as one of the finest patristic scholars of the sixteenth century. What mattered was faithfulness, continuity. Schismatics don't do theology like that.

Calvin's ecclesiology is remarkably high. 'The church is called "catholic" or "universal", because there could not be two or three churches unless Christ be torn asunder [cf I Cor 1:13] – which cannot happen!'[7] That blunt assessment is followed by an exploration of the image of 'mother church' which could have been lifted from the pages of a raft of patristic and medieval writers. 'There is no other way to enter into life unless this mother conceive us in her womb, give us birth, nourish us at her breast, and lastly, unless she keep us under her care and guidance until, putting off mortal flesh, we become like angels [Matt 22:30]' We are pupils in her school for life. Apart from her, there is no forgiveness of sins. It is always 'disastrous' to leave the church. That in turn led to high doctrine of ministry. In his *Commentary on Ephesians* (4:13) Calvin notes, 'The church is the common mother of all the godly, which bears, nourishes, and brings up children to God, kings and peasants alike; and this is done by the ministry.'[8] '...[N]either the light and heat of the sun, nor food and drink, are so necessary to nourish and sustain the present life as the apostolic and pastoral office is necessary to preserve the church on earth.'[9]

The marks of mother church are famously two-fold – 'Wherever we see the Word of God purely preached and heard, and the sacraments administered according to Christ's institution, there, it is not to be doubted, a church exists.'[10] It is a wonderfully generous, ecumenical statement, a paring back to the essential Christological foundations of being church. So generous indeed that at the height of the rhetorical war between Geneva and Rome Calvin recognised church in face of Roman church – '...when we categorically deny to the papists the title of *the* church, we do not for this reason impugn the existence of churches among them.'[11]

So, Calvinist ecclesiology is inherently ecumenical. It can be no other. To be Reformed is, if Calvin's logic is to be followed, simply to be Christian, to be united to Christ through the preaching of the Word and the administration of the sacraments in the fellowship of mother church. Geneva was a small place with a population of c.10-12,000 in Calvin's day, remarkably absorbing an additional 5,000 or so refugees during the reformation years.[12] That may be another clue to Reformed ecumenism. This was not a national church, but the church of an independent city-state. Ecclesiastical self-sufficiency would have been as impossible for the Genevan church as economic or social self-sufficiency. Seeking alliances and networks came naturally.

Reformed ideas and ways of being church spread across Europe, and as they did so they shaped and were shaped by the contingency and flux of politics. Religion in early modern Europe was a tool in the hands of princes and politicians. Territory began to be defined by religion as early as 1531 when the Peace of Kappel recognised the confessional division of the Swiss cantons as Reformed or Catholic. The Peace of Augsburg of 1555 offered German rulers the choice between Catholicism or Lutheranism, deliberately excluding the Reformed and other Protestants in its short-sighted fifth article. That became clear a mere four years later when the Elector Palatine, Friedrich III converted to the Reformed way, thus giving birth to the Heidelberg Confession and establishing Heidelberg as a powerhouse of Reformed thought.[13]

The growth of territorialism in effect proscribed the quest for unity. The imperial peace was far more beguiling to German Lutherans that a common Protestantism. In its turn territorialism fed the growth of confessions which were in part totems of self-definition which worked by anathematising the opposition, so, for example, in its teaching about the eucharist the Lutheran *Formula of Concord* (1580) explicitly condemns the Reformed, both Zwinglian and Calvinist as 'sacramentarians'. Eastern Europe was much more successful in establishing peaceful co-existence between churches – generally because no one church was numerically dominant. Where tolerance was practised in the west, as in the Netherlands, it was essentially pragmatic and within the context of one church being privileged as the state church.

> Stepping beyond confessional boundaries was a dangerous activity. It could result in banishment, imprisonment or worse.

Whatever the internal weaknesses of Reformed theologies of unity, in the crucial formative years of the sixteenth century, political forces determined that the quest for unity was written out of the ecclesiastical agenda. Stepping beyond confessional boundaries was a dangerous activity. It could result in banishment, imprisonment or worse. The infrastructure was set for nationalism and confessionalism. However, that does not exonerate the Reformed tradition, it merely accounts for some of the external forces which shaped its early years.

The internal dynamics of the tradition need examining.

In his last published article, the great Reformed ecumenist Lukas Vischer turned his mind to this problem. Before he turns his mind to ecclesiology, he presents a theologian's view of the historical causes of Reformed fragmentation. First, being Reformed has its origins in the struggle to become the 'true' church. There is something deeply honourable about that, even if we now appreciate that the battle-cry 'ad fontes' leads to a cul-de-sac because there is no one Biblical model of the original 'true' church. To break with Rome and the practices of more than a millennium was an extraordinary thing, deeply shocking, remarkably brave, because it meant re-creating an entire social and theological landscape. If there were no bishops, where did authority lie, and how did ordination happen? If there was no Pope, what was the role of the state in the governance of the church? If there was no magisterium, how were doctrinal debates to be settled? If only God is to be obeyed, and tradition has no weight, how are conflicting interpretations of God's will to be reconciled? As the Reformed negotiated those issues, they arrived at differing conclusions about the nature of church government, the role of the state in the life of the church, doctrine and (eventually) the quest for unity. All of those issues were to lead to schism and disunity.

> If there were no bishops, where did authority lie, and how did ordination happen? If there was no Pope, what was the role of the state in the governance of the church?

Second, Vischer notes, witness leads to schism. The world is indeed 'the theatre of God's glory' (Calvin) and the social order should therefore reflect that glory. The properly wordly spirituality of the Reformed makes them acutely aware of the work of God in the world, and of their political responsibilities. The Barmen Declaration of 1934 and the Belhar Confession of 1986, together with the courage of the Confessing Church in opposing Nazism and the Dutch Reformed Mission Church in the struggle against apartheid underline that Reformed strength. Its obverse is that its commitment to clarity and decisiveness can be myopic. Even if in the short term division is necessary, in the long term it is invariably a cause for lament. Reformed churches have divided on issues of slavery, race, attitudes to dictatorial regimes of both the right and left and other moral issues (for example, the ordination of women). Both these causes of schism are the obverse of strengths.

Vischer's third and fouth reasons are generic and are common to most forms of Protestantism. Missions led to the multiplication of division. Parallel missions by Reformed churches were not co-ordinated and the result has been a diversity of Reformed churches which '...have closer links with their "mother" churches abroad than each other' – a model perpetuated by the impressive missionary passion of the deeply divided Reformed churches of Korea. Closely linked to that in our globalised world is Vischer's fourth reason – the perpetuation of division by migration, illustrated with particular intensity by the proliferation of Dutch, German, Hungarian, and Scottish Reformed churches in the United States. [14]

Despite the present troubles of the Anglican Communion, Anglicans and Lutherans have a more strongly developed sense of communion than the Reformed. So, what is it in Reformed DNA than makes it particularly prone to division?

Vischer isolates three theological genes. The first is the dynamic relationship between Christ and the church, the second freedom, the third the emphasis on the local. It is worth exploring these in a little detail.

For the Reformed the church is created by the Word, but that Word is not static It is spoken by the risen Christ in the power of the Spirit to the church. It is new every morning, dynamic, potent, with the force to bring various Caesars to their knees. It is questing, campaigning, against all those forces that would make God's creation come out wrong. The church is alive with the life of the risen Christ, mediated by the Spirit, not by tradition. That is liberating and exciting, and it is one reason why Reformed ears are so well attuned to the movement of the Spirit in the world, and hence receptive to gifts of human discovery and knowledge.

But that theological emphasis runs a risk. It is as if there is no back story, as if Christ had not spoken new every morning to their fathers and mothers in the faith, as if the communion of saints were limited to present political solidarity. The Reformed have a generous sense of present catholicity, as generous as Calvin's on a good day, but a poor sense of the catholicity which reaches back to the upper room and forwards to the New Jerusalem. If that sense of the body of Christ as an organic entity reaching across space and through time is impaired, the division becomes easier to justify. That, as Vischer shrewdly realises, is intimately related to Reformed attitudes to the eucharist, although he does not explore why.

Reformed liturgists have often reminded us that infrequency should not be mistaken for a lack of seriousness. No one who has studied nineteenth century Scottish communion seasons could doubt that. But, worship shapes spirituality, and a liturgy which centres for most of its time on the transformative, indeed sacramental, power of the Word produces a different spirituality to one in which worshippers are caught up into a continual round of offering, blessing, breaking, and receiving. There is not the least doubt (to my mind) that Christ is really present in both, but to sunder them as the Reformed have done is reductionist. Eucharistic spirituality is at least in part dominated by a sense of being fed by and enfolded into the body of Christ. The experience is corporate and it transcends spatio-temporal limitations as anamnesis collapses past, present and future. A church which is eucharistically focussed might well view schism with more trepidation than one which is not.

A cube of bread cut from a loaf and a thimble of unfermented wine is the Reformed Eucharistic norm. Tailored to the individual. It is the perfect symbol of Vischer's second theological gene – the freedom of the individual. Its theological roots are impeccable. No one stands between Christ and the believer. A mediating priesthood has no place in Reformed thought. Everyone is equal because Christ relates to everyone as they are. Inequalities of gender, class and race have no place in the Christian family because of what God has done in Christ on the cross. That act is politically and anthropologically radical. It creates a new humanity in Christ in which there is neither Jew nor Greek, slave or free. All barriers are transcended, and we are valued equally, each of us, in our genetic uniqueness. That, incidentally, is why

> All barriers are transcended, and we are valued equally, each of us, in our genetic uniqueness.

ecumenism is so important, and that is why the equalities agenda (contra the bishops of the Church of England) is a profoundly Christian agenda. The Reformed believe that every Christian relates to God, and God to every Christian. Together the people of God are his priestly people, lifting the world to God in continual thanksgiving. It is a wonderful vision, and a rich heritage. Its weak obverse is that it encourages individualism, and a way of thinking about the church that begins with individual experience and reflection. The Reformed need the continual reminder of one of their fine hymnwriters, George Matheson that Christian freedom is a paradox, 'Make me a captive Lord, and then I shall be free.' In other words, true uniqueness is only possible in communion.

'Local' is a slippery ecumenical word, referring to a national church, a diocese or the chapel on the corner depending on context. For the Reformed 'local' has always meant the chapel on the corner. Parts of the tradition, particularly the Congregational sub-section, have laid great stress on Christ's promise to be where two or three are gathered (Mt 18:20). There is an elegant simplicity about this understanding of the relationship between Christ and his people. It is particular and local. As the people gather, they do so around the true marks of the church – the preaching of the Word and the administration of the sacraments. Each church is in a direct relationship with Christ. In the best practise of Congregational polity, they are also in relationship with each other, but the true ecclesial reality is the local.

> There is in every expression of church a tension between the local and catholic, but Reformed polity exacerbates it.

There is in every expression of church a tension between the local and catholic, but Reformed polity exacerbates it. Ministry is local, even if you are responsible to presbytery rather than Church Meeting. We do not know that sense of derivation, delegation and sharing which is characteristic of Episcopal ordering and Methodist Connexionalism, and therefore we lack that sense of the church being much more than the local. Anglican and Lutheran churches are not as prone to splintering and schism as we are. Did we throw the catholic baby out with the Episcopal bathwater?

Added together, those three genes render the Reformed susceptible to division. Perhaps the creation of the World Communion of Reformed Churches is evidence that this susceptibility needs addressing and treating. However, the internal dynamics of Reformed theology and its fissiparous tendencies is far from the whole story about the Reformed and ecumenism. The Reformed were proud to be amongst the first advocates of modern ecumenism.

In 1840 a little known theologian called John Williamson Nevin joined the staff of the small German Reformed theological seminary at Mercersburg in Pennsylvania. He was joined four years later by a Swiss church historian from the University of Berlin, Philip Schaff. Schaff was an immensely prolific historian who ended his career loaded

with honour at Union Seminary in New York. Nevin left the
seminary in 1851 to lighten its administrative costs but
stayed in Mercersburg, teaching history at Marshall
College. Between them, for a few heady years in the mid
1840s, they launched what became known as
Mercersburg theology. Schaff's scholarship was
undergirded by the romantic Hegelianism of his teachers.
If the church began on a wave of Petrine objectivity, that
was countered by Pauline freedom and subjectivity, but
the golden age was yet to be in a Johannine synthesis of
love when the work of the reformation would be
completed by synthesising the best of Catholicism and
Protestantism in an age of 'evangelical catholicism'.[15]
Here was a man who thought that the wholesale
multiplication of denominations and sects across
America in the name of religious liberty was a nonsense.
He preached rather a commitment to a world in which
there would be no Catholicism and no Protestantism
'...but an undivided kingdom of God.'[16] Reformed America
was not quite ready for this, but J.W.Nevin was. Nevin was
Charles Hodge's star pupil, but his reading of Calvin took
him to another theological world than that of his
Princeton teacher. His *The mystical presence* (1846) was
a remarkable study which placed union with Christ at the
centre of Calvin's thought, and re-established his
Eucharistic theology. He spoke of Christ's people being
'...inserted by faith into his very life' and of the Lord's
Supper epitomising that mystery. To the 'worthy
communicant' that involved '...an actual participation in
the substance of his person...not simply in his Spirit, but
in his flesh and blood. It is not figurative merely and
moral, but real, substantial and essential.'[17] Poor Charles
Hodge was so appalled that it took him two years to
review the book. It received little attention, but it
anticipated Calvin revisionism by almost a century.

Equally prescient was a sermon which Nevin preached at
the opening of the Triennial Convention of the Reformed
Protestant Dutch and German Reformed Churches at
Harrisburg on August 8th 1844. This was, in a sense, an
ecumenical occasion, so taking as his text Eph 4:4-6,

Nevin launched into an exploration of Christian unity. Mystical union with Christ means that '...Christians of course are vitally related and joined together as one great spiritual whole; and this whole is the Church. The Church is his body, the fulness of Him that filleth all in all.' The unity of the church is, he says, '...a cardinal truth'. To lose it would be to shipwreck the gospel. Sectarianism is '...an immense evil in the church' for '...the spirit of sect and party as such, is contrary to Christ.' Divisions 'disfigure and obscure' the proper glory of the church. What is particularly interesting though is his probing of the relationship between unity and diversity – 'Unity does not exclude the idea of difference and multiplicity. Indeed it is only by means of these, that it can ever appear under an actual, concrete form. Where the one does not carry in itself the possibility of separation and distinction, it can never be more than a sheer abstraction, and absolute nullity. The idea of oneness, however, does require that the different and the manifold as comprehended in it, should be in principle the same, and that all should be held together by the force of this principle actively felt at every point.'[18] In other words, unity is impossible without a proper recognition of legitimate diversity.

Mercersburg offered a different Reformed perspective, a re-connection with Calvin's own passion for the unity of the church. Nevin was not made for the public stage and ecclesiastical politics. Schaff was. In addition to his prolific output, he was an enthusiastic supporter of the formation of the American end of the Evangelical Alliance in 1846, and an energetic advocate of the creation of the World Alliance of Reformed Churches in 1875. But Mercersburg was also part of that flowering of Romanticism which lay behind the Oxford Movement, the Scottish Disruption and the renewal of Lutheranism in Germany.

Ecumenism has long and diverse roots. If Romanticism was one, the Protestant missionary movement was another. That the World Missionary Conference was held in Presbyterian Edinburgh in 1910 is testimony to the Reformed contribution not only to the history of missions, but of the contribution of its missionaries, theologians and administrators to 1910. From Alexander Duff to Joe Oldham, from Lord Balfour of Burleigh to Anne Hunter Small, the list was impressive.[19] Let one, the English Presbyterian missionary John Campbell Gibson, serve as an example of the missionary root of Reformed ecumenism.

He arrived in Swatow, Lingtong, south China as a missionary of in 1874, joining a mission that was 30 years old, a church that had time to put down roots. Gibson was no blinkered fool. He knew full well about the ambiguities and difficulties of being a Western missionary. Like the General Assembly which had sent him, he railed continually against the duplicitous and immoral behaviour of the British government which had not hesitated to use the opium trade as a method of wresting territorial and commercial advantage from the Chinese.[20] He knew from the beginning that he was compromised, yet the imperative of mission led him to spend his working life in China, striving tirelessly from the first for a united Chinese church for the Chinese. It was to be a 'three-self' church, self-governing, self-supporting, self-propagating, and during the 1880s and 1890s he quietly and persistently worked to bring about the structures that would enable that to happen. Speaking at the China Centenary Missionary Conference at Shanghai in 1907 he argued, 'Independence of foreign control is the inherent right of the Chinese Church...[it] will make short work of many of our Western scruples and difficulties. Taught by the Spirit of God dwelling in it as a true member of Christ's Body, it will solve its own questions of organisation and forms of worship, and it will build up its own Theology .' His far-sightedness can be judged from the fact that there were

...he railed continually against the duplicitous and immoral behaviour of the British government which had not hesitated to use the opium trade as a method of wresting territorial and commercial advantage from the Chinese.

only 10 Chinese amongst the 1,170 delegates, and that they were treated as visitors with no vote.[21] The array of Protestant missionary organisations and denominations represented at Shanghai was a bewildering geographical and denominational cat's cradle. Campbell Gibson longed for unity for the Chinese church because disunity was as much a Western import as opium.

It was doubtless that experience that led to his choice as chairman of Commission II on 'The church in the mission field' at the 1910 World Missionary Conference at Edinburgh.[22] His story reveals something of the dynamics behind twentieth-century ecumenism. The first context was the astonishing fecundity of just over a century of Protestant mission. The promise of 'the evangelisation of the world in our generation' seemed not just the pipe-dream of the Student Volunteer Movement for Foreign Missions, but an attainable goal. The second was that missionaries like Gibson were reaching towards a sense that the gospel needed inculturation. Hence Commission II's commendation of a paper from the Shanghai Conference which suggested that the greater challenge to the Chinese church was not ancestor worship but the growth of materialism and atheism amongst the educated. And unity, a church of the Chinese for the Chinese, is an outworking of inculturation.

> The promise of 'the evangelisation of the world in our generation' seemed not just the pipe-dream of the Student Volunteer Movement for Foreign Missions, but an attainable goal.

Gibson's perception was not unique. Bishop Pain of Gippsland, Australia, told the Conference of Anglicans and Presbyterians sitting in council discussing the uniting of their two communions as '...a practical and immediate problem', prompting one contemporary commentator to suggest that '...the latest-born Churches may lead the way for the elder ones towards longed-for unity.'[23]

Since then the contribution of the Reformed to ecumenism has been remarkable. Joe Oldham was, of course, the ubiquitous *eminence grise* working tirelessly behind the scenes at Edinburgh House and in Geneva to craft the conferences and committees that provided the route from Edinburgh to Amsterdam and the creation of the World Council of Churches in 1948. The first two Secretaries of the World Council, Willem Visser t'Hooft and Eugene Carson Blake were both Reformed theologians. Lesslie Newbigin was the General Secretary who from 1959-61 steered the International Missionary Council into integration with the World Council, remaining in Geneva until 1965 as Assistant General Secretary of the Council before returning to India as Bishop of Madras. Those are just the mountain peaks. A sample of the commitment of English Congregationalism to the ecumenical movement can be judged by Donald Norwood's analysis of just one of their theological colleges – Mansfield College, Oxford. A glance around Mansfield's extraordinary chapel, perhaps Basil Champney's finest achievement, reveals a singular catholicity and the saints and scholars of the church catholic in stained glass and statuary surround the worshippers. Mansfield understood at the deepest level that Congregationalism and Catholicism were not in contradiction but rather that the one was the outworking of the other. From W.B. Selbie's presence at Edinburgh 1910 to George Caird's at Vatican II, Mansfield's staff and students made distinguished commitments to the ecumenical movement, and an analysis of their work would show them to have been involved in almost all aspects of British and world ecumenism in the century following 1910.

If Lesslie Newbigin was the public face of the IMC, it was that gentle and most gracious of men, Norman Goodall, who as the London Secretary of the Council for 17 years steered the negotiations between the IMC and the WCC.[24] If Congregationalism was changing, then the work of Nathaniel Micklem, John Whale, Daniel Jenkins, John

Huxtable and the whole Church Order group, which was mainly a Mansfield institution, were the ones helping it to re-ground itself in the theology of the European reformation, and particularly in Calvin. [25]

Unlike Norwood I doubt Mansfield's uniqueness. I suspect that an analysis of major Reformed seminaries across the world would reveal a similar twentieth century pattern, because ecumenism was about the healing of the grievous divisions of a world torn to emotional and spiritual shreds by two world wars. Ecumenism was a way of responding to that, the ecclesial version of truth and reconciliation. Small wonder that so many of the finest Reformed disciples espoused the cause as their own, for we follow one who called himself 'Truth' and who gave his life that God and the world might be reconciled. As Europe began the process of tearing itself apart as the forces of the reformation were unleashed between 1517 and the mid 1540s, John Calvin was deeply aware of the need for reconciliation. He wrote in his commentary on John, '...whenever Christ speaks about unity, let us remember how basely and shockingly, when separated from him, the world is scattered; and, next, let us learn that the commencement of a blessed life is, that we be all governed, and that all live, by the Spirit of Christ alone.'[26] The Reformed ecclesiological journey, passing through political contingency and its own inherent shortcomings, has resulted in a regaining of that vision, albeit shed of its social imperialism.

Now that Europe seems stable and united, Communism has fallen, and American hegemony mightily, if not all, powerful, revisionism strides the land. The modernist, the over-arching, the universal, is out of fashion. The axe is being taken to ecumenical organizations world-wide, and the painstaking work of doctrinal dialogue decried as nothing to do with the reality of mission. Leaving to one side for the moment the embarrassingly difficult question of whether our current pre-occupation with mission is an attempt to distract us from the difficult business of being

Church, we meet in the shadow of a remarkable event, the first State visit of a Pope to these shores since Henry VIII engineered the break with Rome in the 1530s. So neuralgic and difficult has the relationship between England and Rome been, that it spawned a history of persecution, hatred, suspicion and distrust which ran like a seeping sewer through nearly half a millennium. The troubles of Ireland were but one of its offspring. The healing of that division is in some small part to be laid at the door of those patient ecumenists who refused to accept stereotypes or convention because they placed their faith in radical Christian anthropology – that all who belonged to Christ were one in him and sisters and brothers, or at least cousins.

> Be wary then, of revisionists. God knows we Christians have done enough to anathematize and kill in the name of our Lord, and those to whom we would proclaim Christ as Lord have long memories.

Be wary then, of revisionists. God knows we Christians have done enough to anathematize and kill in the name of our Lord, and those to whom we would proclaim Christ as Lord have long memories. Still they do not see us gathered around one table, breaking one loaf, and strangely, they notice such things. Our ecumenical obedience is far from complete. May the Reformed at least not waver from the profound and radically ecumenical conviction that where the word is truly preached and the sacraments truly administered, there indeed is the church of Jesus Christ.

References

1 As quoted in Lucas Vischer *Pia Conspiratorio: Calvin on the unity of the church* (Geneva, John Knox International Reformed Centre 2000) pp 29-30. This work usefully brings together a wide range of Calvin's writings on unity.

2 Frankfurt (1539), Hagenau (1540), Worms and Regensburg (1541)

3 *Op cit* p 40

4 John T McNeil 'Calvin as an Ecumenical Churchman' *Church History* 32 (1963) pp 379-391

5 Alec Ryrie 'Alec Ryrie 'John Calvin in an age of ecumenism:a sketch' *One in Christ* vol 43 no 2 Winter 2009, pp 25-35

6 David Cornick *Letting God be God: the Reformed tradition* (London, Darton, Longman and Todd 2008) p 131

7 I IV.1.3 p 1014

8 I IV.i.4 p 1016

9 I IV.iii.2 p 1055

10 I IV.i..9 p 1023

11 I IV.ii.12 p 1052

12 Bernard Cottret *Calvin – a biography* (ET T & T Clark, Edinburgh 2000) pp 159-60

13 Wim Janse 'Church unity, territorialism, and state formation in the era of confessionalism' in Eduardus van der Borght (ed) *The unity of the church: a theological state of the art and beyond* (Brill, Leiden 2010) pp 33-42; on the short-sightedness of the article see Dairmaid MacCulloch *Reformation: Europe's House divided 1470-1700* (Penguin, London 2003) p 275, 354

14 Lukas Vischer 'Communion, responding to God's gift' in Eduardus van der Borght (ed) *The unity of the church: a theological state of the art and beyond* (Brill, Leiden 2010) pp 19-33; the quotation is at p 24.

15 George Shriver *Philip Schaff: Christian scholar and ecumenical prophet* (Macon, Mercer University Press 1987) p 9 (accessed via Google Books 10.09.10)

16 Brian Gerrish 'J.W.Nevin on the Church and Eucharist' in *Tradition and the modern world: Reformed Theology in the Nineteenth Century* (Chicago, University of Chicago Press, 1978) p. 50

17 John Williamson Nevin *The mystical presence:a vindication of the Reformed or Calvinistic doctrine of the Lord's Supper* (Mercersburg 1846; edn consulted S R Fisher, Philadelphia 1867) p 58 (accessed via Google books 10.10.10)

18 John Williamson Nevin 'Catholic Unity'; www.hornes.org/theologia/john-nevin/catholic-unity – accessed 10.09.10.

19 W.H.T. Gairdner *Edinburgh 1910: an account and interpretation of the World Missionary Conference* (Oliphant, Anderson and Ferrier, Edinburgh and London 1910) pp 53 ff; accessed at www.archive.org, 15.09.10

20 Jonathan D. Spence The search for modern China (London, Hutchinson 1990) pp 204-210 is a nicely judged overview of the ambiguities of the Western mission.

21 Quoted in George Hood Mission accomplished? The English Presbyterian Mission in Lingtung, South China (Frankfurt, Peter Lang, 1986), p 148; Kevin Yao 'At the turn of the century: a study of the China Centenary Missionary Conference of 1907' International Bulletin of Missionary Research (April 2008), accessed 5.05.2010 at http://findarticles.com/p/articles/mi_hb6651/is_200804/ai_n32268300/?tag=content;col1

22 Brian Stanley The World Missionary Conference, Edinburgh 1910 (Grand Rapids, Eerdmans 2009) p 134

23 Gairdner *op cit* p 52

24 DNB, P.R. Clifford; accessed 15.09.10

25 Donald Norwood 'Mansfield and the ecumenical movement' in Tony Tucker (ed) *Mansfield's ministry: a celebration of ordination training at Mansfield College 1886-2009* (URCHS Occasional Publication no 2, 2009)

26 Quoted in Lucas Vischer *Pia Conspiratorio: Calvin on the unity of the church* (Geneva, the John Knox Centre 2000, p 17

A UNITED REFORMED CHURCH PUBLICATION

RENEWING REFORMED THEOLOGY
A Learned ministry for a learned church
David R Peel

"I bring into my theological
investigations scepticism about what
we can know with certainty which
stems from an acute awareness of the
provisionality and relativity of all
human knowledge."

The
United
Reformed
Church

A learned ministry for a learned church...

David R Peel

At a time when I was rather disillusioned about the future of the United Reformed Church I was heartened by a series of articles in *The Journal of the United Reformed Church History Society* written by Martin Camroux, the architect of this conference.[1] What was particularly refreshing was Martin's honesty: "Whether we consider the dream it embodied, its numerical strength, or its identity and vitality, the failure of the United Reformed Church is stark and unmistakable."[2] I had largely come to that conclusion myself after my tour of duty as Moderator of General Assembly (2005-6). A great deal of what I said in my valedictory address as out-going Moderator I found Martin not only echoing but more adequately analyzing.[3] Martin, quite correctly, recognizes that URC failure "can be attributed partly to the general process of secularization", but he then bravely points "to factors specific to the URC".[4] I say 'bravely' because Martin says 'up front' what this supposedly blunt Yorkshire man on the Assembly platform had only had the courage to express in rather coded language. The URC-specific driving forces of our decline, according to Martin, have been "the disastrous collapse of [our] ecumenical dream ... theological poverty, and ... failure to find any significant motivating purpose".[5] And it's the second of those particular failures which no doubt has been the reason for holding this conference about 'Renewing Reformed Theology'. After all, there's no point in renewing things if they are working well!

My particular contribution to this conference is to ask theologically what it means today to say that central to what is needed to drive us beyond failure towards renewed identity and fresh vision is a 'learned' ministry. I share with Martin a 'bottom-up' understanding of the church in which everything outside the local church in denominational life should exist to serve each local out-cropping of gathered saints in their mission. An institutional form beyond the local is needed to underpin a genuine sense of catholicity in our ecclesial shape, but it is clear (to me at least) that the purpose of the 'wider' church is largely given in what it provides for the 'local' church. Among that provision, I believe, is a ministry which animates and resources a 'learning' church. What I mean by 'learning church' is somewhat akin to what Martin Camroux describes as "theologically active local congregations with a vision of what the gospel is and a delight in it and the conviction that 'The Lord has yet more light and truth to break forth from his word'."[6]

What I mean by 'learning church' is somewhat akin to what Martin Camroux describes as "theologically active local congregations with a vision of what the gospel is and a delight in it and the conviction that 'The Lord has yet more light and truth to break forth from his word'."

It follows that an important consideration in my reflections concerns the relationship between those called to exercise their designated ministries within and for congregations and all those church members who through their own baptism have been endowed with unique vocations in the *missio dei*. A lot of discussion in the church regrettably oscillates between, on the one hand, so stressing the ordained and commissioned ministries of the church that the vocations of church members get devalued, and, on the other hand, that understandable championing of the vocations of those mistakenly called 'laity' which slowly and surely ends up robbing our ordained and commissioned servants of their *raison d'être*.[7] What I am searching for is an ecclesiology which liberates church members to exercise their vocations without undermining the crucial way in which ordained and commissioned roles can and should contribute to the church's *bene esse*.

It is often the case that teachers over-estimate their influence on those they teach and under-estimate what they have learnt from others. A quick investigation of a theologian's teachers will often tell you most of what you need to know about their line of thinking. That is as true of the more seminal thinkers as it is of people like me who hang on to their coat-tails. "Honour your sources", one of my teachers thundered when he found me saying something I had obviously unwittingly 'borrowed' from one of the great and good. So I will mention Schubert Ogden, since it was that particular theologian who taught me that the *prolegomena* to theological investigation is the most significant part of all such enquiry.[8] Where one starts will largely determine one's destination; who one talks to on the journey will greatly influence what one decides to say; and who one intends to communicate with will generally shape the scope of the investigation. Then there is the thorny issue of what weight is given to different sources of information placed before the theologian: scripture, tradition, experience and reason. Where, indeed, does one begin? The answer is by a humble recognition that there is no neutral starting point and then getting on with the matter.

The Significance of Context

We should never underestimate the constraints and opportunities of contextuality. It sets limits to what we can know as well as provides vantage points unique to each of us. Where I have come from and the companions with whom I have chosen to share the theological journey have highly influenced the transitory destination at which I have arrived. If I had been born female or black I may have come to a different place; while if I had not trained as a scientist I perhaps would not have asked people so often: "How do you know that is the case?" Nor perhaps would I have distressingly found great swathes of Christian writing largely beside what I perceive to be the point. I bring into my theological investigations scepticism about what we can know with certainty which stems from an acute awareness of the provisionality and relativity of all human knowledge. This need not represent a descent into a woolly form of liberalism; but it most certainly does mean that, given the relativity of all our thinking, we will need the insights of others so that together we can journey on to a fresh destination, one which is different to the one we were respectively occupying before engaging in a mutual search for understanding and truth.

Human psychology, gender, cultural background, race, even genetic make-up and so on, affect the way we think and thereby the theological conclusions at which we arrive; but, I believe, they do not necessarily determine it. When a women colleague rounds on me, saying: "Well, David, you would think that, you're a man", I am prone to take that conclusion as an invitation to invite her to show me how my conclusions have become warped due to my gender. But, regrettably I have sometimes discovered that such comments are intended to be the end of the discussion. It is sad when those who see very clearly the non-theological factors which influence other people's theology end up adopting absolutist positions seemingly more impregnable than those they originally so perceptively unmasked as ideological!

It may be the case that the non-theological factors thrown up by our inevitable contextuality are sometimes the hidden driving force for our Christian theology and practice. I am not alone in having observed the way in which some theological opinions upon inspection largely seem to serve the interests and comforts of those who hold them. All this is rather easy to see when 'the great and good' are caught falling from grace. Vincent J. Donovan, I guess, speaks for all of us: "The god invoked by the pope to bless the troops of Mussolini about to embark on the plunder of Ethiopia, and the god invoked by an American cardinal to bless the 'soldiers of Christ' in Vietnam, and the god of French glory, and the German god of Hitler were no more the High God of scripture than is Diana of the Ephesians' or Engai of the Masai of East Africa."[9] Less easy to see, though, is the way in which some ecclesiological debates in the church often reveal the self-interests of the participants. Nowhere is that more obvious than in discussions about ministerial training.

In 2006 I represented the United Reformed Church at the General Assembly of the Church of Scotland. The two controversial topics on the agenda were somewhat familiar to me: first, whether or not the Kirk should ordain homosexuals who are in life-long relationships; and, secondly, whether or not the Kirk was prepared to validate another theological college to prepare men and women for ordination in addition to the long-established University-based colleges. The debate on ordaining practising homosexuals was a carbon copy of similar debates in other churches. The debate about validating an additional theological college interested me more, partly because of my involvement in theological education but also partly because the Church of Scotland was proposing to increase the educational establishments available to its ordinands at the very time the URC was moving in the opposite direction. It was a long debate with many of the distinguished academics in the Kirk holding court. Their fears were made clear: Would the new college maintain the present standards of theological training? The major argument in favour of validating another college was that its position in the Highlands would provide easier access for ordinands from Highland parishes. The academics lost the day and the Highland Theological College was validated. But, sometime after the debate, I realized that underneath the debate were two largely unspoken factors. One concerned the perceived theological hue of the Highland College: it was 'evangelical'. And I do not think I misrepresent many of those speaking in favour of validating it on the grounds

Human psychology, gender, cultural background, race, even genetic make-up and so on, affect the way we think and thereby the theological conclusions at which we arrive; but, I believe, they do not necessarily determine it.

of 'access' if I suggest that they were mostly conservative evangelicals. The second largely unspoken factor concerned the survival of the ancient colleges if another institution came on the scene. In recent debates in the United Reformed Church we have been rather more open about concentrating resources in our 'ancient' institutions. Unlike the Church of Scotland we have reduced the number of our validated institutions to protect 'our' own, but not without hinting at a fear that in some ecumenical institutions our candidates were being overwhelmed by non-Reformed practices and sensibilities.

The URC approach to theological colleges may turn out to be a case study that arguably confirms what Martin Camroux describes as the disastrous collapse of our ecumenical dream. Have we not moved from enthusiastic commitment to an involvement in The Queen's College in Birmingham and participation in various ecumenical courses to a concentration of our activity in ex-Congregational and Presbyterian colleges whose ecumenical relations are federal rather than organic in nature? But whatever the answer, I cannot avoid asking myself whether my thinking about ordination provision has been as self-servingly motivated as, from a distance, appeared that of the Kirk's academics. Was I always really interested in the best ordination preparation for our URC candidates? Or might I have been more motivated, even if unwittingly, to feather my nest and help protect the institution for which I was working, whether that was Northern College or NEOC? Or perhaps it was the case, or I had been tempted to believe it was, that the survival of the institution I served was in fact *the* way to get the best ordination preparation for URC candidates? There are clear vested interests in

> Was I always really interested in the best ordination preparation for our URC candidates? Or might I have been more motivated, even if unwittingly, to feather my nest and help protect the institution for which I was working...?

every discussion about theological education and I suspect that sometimes we have allowed them to warp our sense of direction.

The Nature of Theology

One of the tasks of the Christian theologian is to expose the non-theological factors that distort our thinking and practice. Theology essentially is a process of *critical* reflection on Christian witness and practice. It interrogates what Christians are saying and doing to achieve two things: (1) to judge whether or not the witness and practice is faithful to the Jesus tradition, as that is normed for us by Scripture and has been replicated at the best moments in Christian history; and (2) to determine whether or not the witness and practice is credible in the contemporary world. There are two criteria of theological adequacy, not one: not just *appropriateness* to the Jesus tradition (as that is set in the context of the religion of Israel as its precursor and the church which flowed from it, and hence tied to Scripture), but also *credibility* in the world within which the church is set where, through Godly persuasion and Spiritual prompting, human beings in different cultures have gained in experience and developed in knowledge – sometimes for the better even if sometimes for the worse. What we learn from historiography, political theory and the natural as well as the social sciences means that Christians of one age may well disagree with the witness of their predecessors, even though there always will be some in denial about the way secular knowledge impacts on Christian theology.

If the first moment of theological thinking is a process of critical reflection, the second is the constructive activity of establishing what an appropriate and credible contemporary Christian praxis involves and entails. This is achieved by engendering an interaction between the 'givenness' of the Jesus tradition (and hence the scripture that norms it and the Christian traditions that seek to replicate it) and the 'givenness' of what the contemporary culture believes to be the case and accepts as good practice. The outcome of this theological interaction then becomes the latest Christian witness and practice we are then to adopt. Since our perception of what constitutes the Jesus tradition is always subject to fresh insights from our engagement with Scripture and learning the lessons of Christian history what we bring to the theological interaction from that particular side will always be as subject to change as what is brought there from the other side generated from contemporary thinking and many a culture. We are never in the position of applying an unchanging Gospel to a changing world, since, as the history of Christianity shows, what is perceived as an unchanging Gospel is actually subject to change, and hence there is potential for change on *both* sides of the theological interrogation. The result is that the theological task is ongoing; the critical task and creative construction never end; and the theological roots of *ecclesia reformata, semper reformanda* have thus been laid bare.

It is precisely this understanding of theology which I generally find absent in so much of the life of the United Reformed Church. A recognition that what we say and do should be made subject to critical enquiry from *both* the side of scripture and tradition *as well as* from the side of all that human enquiry and experience has given us – this recognition is somewhat scarce in both pulpit and pew. Indeed, it is positively eschewed by those among us who, in the name of 'true' Reformed theology, reject what they see as the encroachment of liberal theology on their avowed 'orthodoxy', 'neo-orthodoxy' or 'new orthodoxy'. They see Calvin and Barth as their heroes, and thus want to brand Friedrich Schleiermacher as the black-sheep within the Reformed family. It was Schleiermacher, you will recall, who is credited with being the founding father of liberal theology; it was, note, a Reformed theologian who unleashed protestant liberalism: not an Anglican, not a Lutheran, not a Methodist, but a Reformed minister theologian! It is not his conclusions that are significant so much as the fact that he believed that through God's grace we all have things to learn from beyond the

Christian circle and that theology is more open, adventurous and, hence, risky than we might have been led to believe from those who believe it to be a form of enquiry self-contained within the circle of faith.

The future of Reformed theology can be put in the form of a question: Do we believe there is one criterion for theological adequacy or two? Do we acknowledge that the world beyond the church might have a few things to contribute to Christian understanding, things even that might qualify or question inherited Christian understandings that have evolved during the history of the church, even perhaps the 'taken for granted' certainties of those who made up the earliest groups within the Jesus movement? Let me put it in other words: the way we go theologically as a Reformed family will be determined largely by whether or not we believe the world and the church belong in a critical-engagement in which the

> We are never in the position of applying an unchanging Gospel to a changing world, since, as the history of Christianity shows, what is perceived as an unchanging Gospel is actually subject to change, and hence there is potential for change on both sides of the theological interrogation.

truth does not totally rest on *either* side, and whether we recognize that sometimes the church becomes the partner in need of most learning. The theological basis for this rests in the belief that God is the God of the *whole* world and not a sectarian deity of the church; or to put it another way, God's work is not confined to the Christ event, so much as defined by it. To go back to personalities: Did Barth really sound the death-knell for liberal theology? Or is Barth's theological contribution better seen as a self-critical moment within the history of liberal theology, a reminder that however much theological liberals wish to speak relevantly and coherently to the age they must be wary of so reducing Christian faith and practice to what is acceptable that it is no longer authentically Christian?

It is my conviction that the failure of the mainstream churches, in general, and the United Reformed Church, in particular, is rooted in their reluctance to embrace both the *critical* and *constructive* challenges of their theological task. To caricature somewhat: the conservatives through their lack of critical spirit end up in obscurantism, while the liberals get so caught up with their critical spirit that they never seem to get round to constructing alternatives. We all need to recapture the vision that drove Schleiermacher to address 'the cultured despisers', not least because there's a world of *them* now outside the church door; just as much as we need to rediscover from scripture an understanding of being the church largely lost in many of our congregations.

The kind of church for which we need ministers

One way of summarizing the church's plight is to say that we preach a lot and we do a lot, but we don't think a lot. As a result, what we say and do makes little impact on the outside world. The reason is not just that we do not have the ability at grass-root's level to address the world's questions; it also concerns the way we have allowed our church culture to hide, even distort, the Jesus tradition. Outside one hour each Sunday, most of what happens in many of our churches has little obvious connection with the Jesus tradition that motivated the earliest churches. The vital kingdom-orientated message and practice has become hidden inside an institution about whose survival we are so desperately concerned, but whose demise in some places might turn out to be the most Godly of eventualities. The only rationale for ecclesial development that carries a biblical mandate is one shaped by the process of 'death leading to resurrection', but we are very reluctant to face up to the

> The only rationale for ecclesial development that carries a biblical mandate is one shaped by the process of 'death leading to resurrection'

temporality and hence finiteness of the historical manifestations of the church.

URC discussions have often been skewed by our inability to trade off our inherited loyalties to the Churches of Christ, Congregational and Presbyterian traditions against our ecumenical sensitivities which drive us to embrace those from other parts of the Christian family. But if one of the criteria of adequacy concerning what it means to be a church predates each and every denomination and the other lies outside them, then the really crucial question is simply: How do we fulfil our calling to be a faithful church?

When Martin Camroux concludes that it is hard "to justify the existence of a separate denomination on the basis of David Peel's ecclesiology"[10] he unwittingly delivers a compliment, because any seriously radical theology has to conclude that nothing flowing from the Jesus tradition can justify any denomination – we are all followers of Jesus, for God's sake; and then further there is not a scrap of evidence that anybody outside the church is interested one jot in commitment to a denomination, when what today counts is a welcoming community of God's saints who offer a style of being church they happen to need – or at least want. Traditional 'brand' loyalties count for little in the ecclesial market place, particularly when they do not offer what they say on the tin.

We hardly need to document why there is so much distrust of institutional religion. It always is easier to look with pity upon Anglicans and Roman Catholics coping with their alleged misogyny and homophobia than it is to unlock the skeletons in our Reformed cupboards. Whether one looks at the contemporary mainstream churches in the West from the perspective of the Jesus tradition, or from that governed by common experience and reason, it is pretty obvious that they are in acute difficulty. The really damaging thing is that the spiritual searchers of our age have to claw their way through the church before they can reach the God who yearns to embrace them in the life and work of Jesus and through the Spirit. Most of course quickly lose the energy to succeed.

At the risk of echoing an analogous, if often misunderstood, programme associated with the name of Rudolf Bultmann, paying close attention to our origins as a church ought to cause us to want to de-institutionalise the church and re-configure it missiologically.[11] And just as Bultmann never intended us to under-value the power and point of 'myth' in our lives, neither ought we to pretend that the church can ever be free of an institutional framework. We know full well in the Reformed world that when two or three gather in Jesus' name not only is he in the midst but we have also inevitably formed a committee to disagree over what God is saying to us; we also know that when the three became thirty of us we will need a larger place to meet then Fred's front room; and then soon we will need a treasurer...; and so it goes on! But surely we cannot countenance what has been bequeathed to us? It borders on the absurd for us now to be as concerned with our inherited institutional shape as we seem to be when Western society is driven by social networking and is eschewing membership of all institutions.

It is always easier to work *in* the church than it is to engage with others *outside* it as we attempt to live out Jesus' kingdom vision. Do we really want to go on preparing men and women for ordained and commissioned roles in the church when the wooden if egalitarian way we deploy them often means they inevitably will only ever be able to manage our decline and, in effect, perform the task of institutional bereavement counsellors. Perhaps we do? Our pastoral responsibilities to existing congregations may actually demand just that! But we also urgently need those who can lead the church beyond its current institutionalized demise to help the gathered saints re-configure themselves in fresh ways for mission.

Our Missiological Context

The kind of ministry most needed in these challenging times is one which will enable us to move beyond our *centripetal* tendencies towards more *centrifugal* ways. Christians need to re-learn that life faithful to the gospel requires them to turn outwards to engage with God in a kingdom-building project rather than propagate a mentality which seems obsessed about institutional survival. We would do well to apply Jesus' existential challenge to all our ecclesiastical activities: "For those who want to save their life will lose it, and those who lose their life for my sake, and for the sake of the gospel, will save it" (Mk 8: 35 and ff). Inward concerns about the church are only justified in so far as they serve the institutional requirement to provide the setting and the resources for worship, teaching and fellowship to equip us for our missionary adventure. We do not need to concur with all the late Lesslie Newbigin thought and said but we neglect at our peril the missionary centrality of his ecclesiology.[12] As Newbigin insisted, "a church which is not 'the church of mission' is no church at all".[13] His vision of the gathered saints, called to be a sign and sacrament of God's reign over all things, places the universal *missio dei* in localities not congregations.[14] To suggest the reverse is to confuse the end for which the church exists with the means to bring it about. And we need a ministry which by declared intent as well as living example helps us get things the right way round.

> ...we need a ministry which by declared intent as well as living example helps us get things the right way round.

On the face of it, some may find it odd that I am labouring the point about mission providing the church with its *raison d'être*. They will point out that there is a greater emphasis on mission in the contemporary church than in recent times. Hasn't it been accepted for some time now, they will say, that the post-Christian West is the mission-field on our doorstep? And, the objectors will continue, haven't you read *Mission-shaped Church*[15], and do you not recognize the many ways in which faithful folk are creating 'fresh expressions' of being church? My simple answer is that I am aware of all this and I am engaged with it. I have read the book – perhaps with more critical eyes than some others; and I am very supportive of genuine attempts to be the church in seemingly 'non-churchy' ways. But I find that when I investigate all the contemporary 'mission-speak' and related activity it turns out very often to be nothing at all directly to do with the *missio dei* and everything instead to do with the survival of the church.

John M. Hull's critique of the Anglican report, *Mission-shaped Church*, that has stimulated so much recent interest is under forty pages, but it was sold at such an exorbitant price that it turned out to be penny per word just about the most expensive bit of theological reading I have undertaken. Yorkshire men want value for money, so imagine my amazement when after reading Hull's brief piece all consideration of cost had vanished – well almost! On the basis of an ecclesiology identical to that of Newbigin, Hull takes to task *Mission-shaped Church* for "its failure to distinguish clearly between church and the mission of God, and consequently its limited ecclesiology and its restricted view of the scope of the Christian mission".[16] He lays bare the fact that a whole lot of what goes on entitled 'mission' is actually nothing of the sort; rather, it is all about 'church'. Where we all go horribly wrong is that we do not recognize that "the correct distinction is between the church as an agent and the Kingdom as a goal"[17] Hull's concluding words at the close of an extremely persuasive critique reveals not just the lacunae of *Mission-shaped Church* but also problems within the Church of England:

...what we have is a lament over the broken territorialism of the Church of England; a church that sees in its mission little more than the creation of more and more churches, one that manifests an inability to perceive the church through the lens of Christian faith, a church that patronizes the poor, that ignores diversity, clings to an imperial past, and which most disturbing of all is innocent. We looked for a mission-shaped church but what we found was a church-shaped mission.[18]

John Hull is physically blind, but we can thank God that he can see; and we need ministers who can see as clearly as him!

Perhaps the most difficult thing a 'mission-shaped' church has to realize is that it has far less to contribute in its engagement with the world than it thinks and far more to learn from the world than it is prepared to accept. Mission is always a two-way street. We become our first converts as we engage with the *missio dei*. However much it is most certainly true that mission involves the church calling and cajoling persons and systems to adopt Christ-shaped goals and values, it is also true that the church will be challenged to re-shape itself as it encounters God already at work in the world. Few have seen this as clearly as Vincent J. Donovan and few have written about mission more endearingly than this seminal Roman Catholic missionary to East Africa. He has certainly identified where Western Christianity has arrived:

What we have to be involved in is not the revival of the church or the reform of the church. It has to be nothing less than ... the refounding of the Catholic church for our age.[19]

But, as Donovan insists, the goal is not the church – Catholic or Reformed; it is something far greater, not to be found in the church so much as when the church breaks itself open in Eucharistic action for the world; never a possession but always a gift:

> The experience of discovery such as I am describing is rather more like the loneliness of a person who has climbed to a mountain peak and sees spread out around him the most beautiful panoramic vision and vista and finds it completely impossible to describe that vision, or even to discuss it, except with someone who agrees to climb that peak in turn.[20]

And we need ministers who have been to the mountain top and who return to take others there but have the humility to recognize that those they take there will see things they have missed. Then the church will be re-created. What might start as a church-shaped mission will end in a mission-shaped church as people discover the freshness and vitality of God's vision for the world. And we need ministers to become the practical guides who enable those mission-shaped churches who do learn what the gospel is really about then to share and live it with others:

> ...do not try to call them to where you are, as beautiful as that place might seem to you. You must have the courage to go with them to a place that neither you nor they have ever been before.[21]

And that new-found place will be where God-in-mission has gone before us.

Most of us going on a journey, though, like the security provided by a reliable map. As the Spirit propels us out of the church to engage in the *mission dei* what kind of world are we encountering in Britain? It seems generally agreed that we are in the midst of a social and cultural sea-change in which all the features of a previous age seem to be on the wane. But we do not know what of Christendom will remain in *post*-Christendom – although I suspect it will be rather more than the proponents of the 1960's secularization thesis expected; nor do we know how much of liberalism will remain in a *post*-liberal world – although I suspect it will be rather more than religious fideists would like, since the practice of submitting human judgments before the prevailing canons of reason and experience is hardly likely to be given up in a hurry.[22] We live between the times, rather akin, formally if not materially, to those who first heard Jesus' call upon them to make a radical decision about how they were going to live.

As the old religious certainties and institutions rock in the prevailing wind, what are those searching for meaning and purpose going to receive? Clearly, there are many alluring fundamentalisms in the shop window, some scientific, some hedonistic, many religious. All we have to offer, though, is the person who is a presence

> It seems generally agreed that we are in the midst of a social and cultural sea-change in which all the features of a previous age seem to be on the wane.

as well as a power: the God of Abraham and Sarah and the Lord Jesus Christ, the relativizer of all absolutes, who gave birth to a community called 'church' set apart to serve the over-riding purpose of divine kingdom-building. In order to get in proper shape that community ought to pay due attention to the 'signs of the times': a deep-seated suspicion of authority; a dismissal of those whose claims are not matched by their deeds; a determination to have personal agendas' addressed; a fear of centralist power and structures and a preference for local decision-making and delivery. This prevailing *Zeitgeist* sits very uneasily with church leaders who traditionally have stood ten feet above contradiction; church structures that are hierarchical by design on the basis of a conviction that that is how God has ordained things: clergy abuse and the systemic cover-up of it; the habitual propensity of the church to be found preaching a great deal and listening very little; and churches following the prevailing patterns of ailing organisations by seeking centralist solutions to all their problems. The church can learn a great deal from the age it so often speaks judgmentally about, and, ironically, it may in the process rediscover the value of some of the things that defined the earliest Christian communities.

I have used the word 'learning' as if it is a self-explanatory term, when, of course, it is highly controversial. Education, like theology, comes with a lot of hidden baggage. If you don't believe me then listen next Easter to the different takes on the current educational scene that are given by spokespersons at the various teacher union conferences; or if you prefer to have the hidden baggage conveyed in more sophisticated code compare the utterances of the officials of the Russell Universities with those of the rest of the Higher Education sector. Similar ideologically loaded dialogues have been experienced between those who work in university departments of theology and those who staff theological training courses. In the former the intellectual component of theological development holds sway. The theological conclusions drawn from one's studies are not expected necessarily to alter how one chooses to live one's life, nor do they have any intrinsically necessary bearing on one's spiritual condition. In a theological college, on the other hand, practical and spiritual dimensions of human development come much higher up the priority scale. There is a great deal of evidence to suggest that quite often in our preparation of men and women for ordination it has been the 'intellectualist' university paradigm which has dominated our assessment processes. The formation required of Christians most certainly concerns the development of intellectual acumen, but it is equally concerned with the acquisitions of skills and, of course, spiritual development. We do church members a disservice if we place before them ministers who, through dysfunctonality in one or other of the three dimensions of learning, are far from being integrated disciples of Jesus Christ.

Ministry

In his classic book, *What Prevents Christian Adults from Learning?*, John M. Hull argues that the twin aims of Christian Education are "to let the past speak" and "let the future be".[23]

Only then will we come near to understanding the present in a way that we can inhabit it with confidence. Christian education involves our minds, hearts and wills in cultivating a Christian *habitus* or disposition which bears the marks of God: Creator, Redeemer and Sustainer.[24] Such education is the duty of all Christians and it ought not to be a threat but an ongoing delight for us. But an enthusiastic commitment to life-long learning seems to be largely missing from many parts of the church. And I have not known it any different.

One of the very first theological books I read as a teenager was Mark Gibbs and T. Ralph Morton's *God's Frozen People: A book for – and about – ordinary Christians*. It carries a sustained plea that ordinary folk should take hold of their vocational gifting, play their full parts in the kingdom-shaping work of the church, and thus break down the clericalism to which the churches are beholden.[25] The book had a profound impact upon me in that it put in place a conviction at an early age that while Christian discipleship and vocation is universally shared among the gathered saints, everyone is not called to be a 'designated' minister within the church; or, to put the matter another way round, the fact that God calls certain people to be 'designated' ministers within the church does not mean that they are the only ones in the church who have Christian vocations. Looking back I can recognize now the influence this book had in my discovering a 'call' to be a minister. It may seem rather odd to some that a book devoted to awakening lay men and women to take up their Christian vocations should propel me down the path of ordination. But what the book also taught me was that the chief responsibility of an ordained minister is to support, encourage and equip church members in their vocations. We act on the church, so that church members can act in and for the world.[26] That was what excited me about becoming a minister.

Looking back it is hardly surprising that I have at times borne frustrations since my ordination. As minister of a local church in three different settings I have been fighting the same prevailing church culture that came under the critical eye of the authors of *God's Frozen People*. Not only did the years of plenty in Nonconformity provide the funding for numbers of stipendiary ministers that the current times of famine cannot afford, but it also generated a view that ministry is provided from outside the church rather than generated from within it. Even in traditions one might have expected to have known better and modelled more realistic and relevant patterns of ministry, the fact remains that, irrespective of the on-going presence of elders and deacons in their lives, the absence of a stipendiary minister was often taken to be akin to the absence of ministry. This fact was psychologically underscored in many a church through the provision of an interim moderator to lead them through what was once, horrifically, called an interregnum or, little better, is now called a vacancy. But we are prone to forget that even in the years of plenty, there was many a healthy nonconformist chapel which carried on quite faithfully without ordained leadership, even though the feeling might have been that this fact made them second-class citizens in a competitive non-conformist market place.

When the proposals for the United Reformed Church were debated, it was not unusual in the Congregational Churches of the North of England for what was being proposed to gain support for reasons totally unrelated to any form of ecumenical vision. The Scheme of Union guaranteed stipendiary ministry to each church, along with central payments of ministers on a much higher scale than the Congregational minimum stipend. 'Ministers for every church' and 'higher stipends' (no longer dependent upon the level of local church giving) were the driving force for accepting the Scheme of Union in many places. Viewed 'bottom-up' what strikes me now is how progressively ecumenical things are in some of those same places! Viewed 'top-down' the URC project might need writing off as a failure, but applying a 'bottom-up' analysis one is driven to recognize that we are actually more ecumenical now than we were in 1972. This in turn prompts the thought that the United Reformed Church perhaps does not present a case study representing the failure of ecumenism so much as, at its best, a pointer to the way the Spirit leads people to suspect uniform Christian belief and practice as well as centralist patterns of ecclesial life, and, at our worst, the way the Spirit weaves the ecumenical cloth out of all too human, self-interested threads.

> Sociologists of a rather anti-church hue somewhat gleefully suggest that we have only managed to get this far without the system collapsing by introducing a category of ministers to do the same work free of remuneration.

Be that as it may, nearly forty years down the line, we face the difficulty of squaring a circle: on the one hand, we have the insatiable desire of congregations for stipendiary ministry and, on the other hand, as the famine cuts deeper, we find that we simply cannot afford the ministers the churches demand. Sociologists of a rather anti-church hue somewhat gleefully suggest that we have only managed to get this far without the system collapsing by introducing a category of ministers to do the same work free of remuneration. I have a rather deeper appreciation of self-supporting ministers than that, but the fact remains that they still remain second best in the eyes of many a church member and constantly report that they are treated as inferior by some of their stipendiary colleagues.

In recent discussions about ministry there have been two elephants in the room: one named 'ordination' and the other called 'stipend'. Our prevailing ecclesial culture is one in which the work of the church is largely viewed through a paradigm centred upon the ordained within the *laos* rather than one focussed on the vocations of the whole *laos*. When we refer to the 'ordained' most usually think of 'ministers'. Only seldomly do we take into account the team of ordained men and women at the heart of our congregations who make up the Elders' Meeting. On the surface at least, it is hard to equate our problems with a lack of 'ordained' persons. The prevailing church culture also is hot-wired with the idea that stipendiary ministers are normative and, to use an earlier somewhat revealing description, non-stipendiary ministers are *auxiliary* to them. That idea finds little or no support in any of the foundational examples of the church in the biblical period; it is an idea of a remarkably recent generation; and it cannot be financially sustained. The more our churches look outside themselves for ministry the more they are going to be disappointed. When they free themselves from their addiction to a somewhat modern paradigm they will discover that, if the Spirit wants them to have life, most of what they need will be discovered from within. Or, to put it rather crudely: You see, that's what Elders are for, isn't it?[27]

The more our churches look outside themselves for ministry the more they are going to be disappointed.

That leaves us with a smaller number of stipendiary ordained and commissioned servants that we will be able to afford. What may essentially be a financially induced inevitability however could well drive us back to more theologically appropriate patterns of church leadership. Fewer can mean more, if the few along with self financed colleagues can mentor and resource Elders in such a way that Elders become confident in their leadership roles in the Chair of Church Meeting and behind the Lord's Table, having been equipped theologically, skilfully and spiritually to lead the faithful in their vocations within the *missio dei*. Fewer can also mean more, when the few equip Church Members to be confident in the sharing of their faith, to be politically astute as they seek to mould their communities in Kingdom-shaped ways, and to open the church out as a fellowship of acceptance and love to the least of our Lord's brothers and sisters. Ministers of Word and Sacrament, Church Related Community Workers and Evangelists could thus become available to several congregations, once it was accepted that the day to day responsibilities for local church life rested solely with the Elders. The demands upon the candidates for all our designated ministries should be high – they need to be 'learned' in the holistic sense I have mentioned, with 'mentoring' and 'educational' skills matching their grasp of the Christian tradition and their firm spiritual foundation.

References

[1] See "Why did the United Reformed Church Fail?" in *The Journal of the United Reformed Church History Society* (JURCHS), 8, 1 (Jan.2008), 30-45; 8, 2 (May 2008), 99-159; 8, 3 (Dec. 2008), 138-149; 8, 4 (June 2009), 210-225.

[2] Martin Camroux, "Why did the United Reformed Church Fail?" in *JURCHS*, 8, 1 (Jan.2008),30.

[3] See my *Encountering Church* (London, The United Reformed Church, 2006), 113-119.

[4] Camroux, "Why did the United Reformed Church Fail: 1?", 30.

[5] *Ibid.*

[6] Camroux, "Why did the United Reformed Church Fail: 4?", *JURCHS*, 8, 4 (June 2009), 224-5

[7] The church is the people (*laos*) of God and, as such, those who undertake ordained and commissioned roles within it are just as much part of the 'laity' as are the rest of the gathered saints!

[8] The theologian in question is Schubert M. Ogden. For his account of what is involved in theological enquiry see *On Theology* (San Francisco: Harper & Row, Publishers, 1986) and *Doing Theology Today* (Valley Forge, PA: Trinity Press International, 1996).

[9] Vincent J. Donovan, *Christianity Rediscovered: An Epistle from the Masai*, 3rd end. (London: SCM Press, 2001), 37.

[10] Camroux, "Why did the United Reformed Church fail: 3?", 144.

[11] For an account of Bultmann's programme of 'demythologizing' and 'existential re-interpretation' see Rudolf Bultmann, *Jesus Christ and Mythology* (New York: Charles Scribner's Sons, 1958) and *New Testament and Mythology and Other Basic Writings* (London SCM Press, 1985). Bultmann was saddened by the many mistaken interpretations of his work and became particularly annoyed at some of the English language critiques. Notable exceptions were found by him in the writings of Ronald Gregor Smith and Schubert M. Ogden. For a , if critical, outline of Bultmann's basic theological position see Schubert M. Ogden's 'Introduction' in *Existence and Faith: Shorter Writings of Rudolf Bultmann* (London: Fontana, 1964), 9-23.

[12] See my "The Theological Legacy of Leslie Newbigin" in Anna M. Robbins, ed. *Ecumenical and Eclectic: The Unity of the Church in the Contemporary World. Essays in Honour of Alan P.F. Sell* (Milton Keynes: Patrnoster, 2007), 129-148.

[13] Lesslie Newbigin, *The Open Secret: Sketches for a Missionary Theology* (Grand Rapids, Michigan: William B. Eerdmans Publishing Company, 1978).

14 The influence of Lesslie Newbigin on the ecumenical life of the church is well-known. *In God's Reign and Our Unity: The Report of the Anglican-Reformed International Commission 1981-1884* (London: SPCK and Edinburgh: The Saint Andrew Press, 1984), 9, we find the central ethos of the report described as follows: "Our Report is written in the conviction that the Church is to be understood ... as a pilgrim people called to a journey whose goal is nothing less than God's blessed Kingdom embracing all nations and all creation, a sign, instrument and foretaste of God's purpose 'to sum up all things with Christ as head' (Eph. 1:10)". That is pure Newbigin – hardly surprising given that there is every likelihood that he helped draft the Report!

15 *Mission-shaped Church: Church Planting and Fresh Expressions of Church in a Changing Context* (London: Church House Publishing, 2004).

16 *Ibid.*, 1..

17 *Ibid.*, 3.

18 *Ibid.*, 3b.

19 Donovan, *op.cit.*, XIX

20 *Ibid.*,2.

21 The strategy of "a young person in an American University" as recorded by Donovan, op.cit., XIX

22 The sociological analysis of religion in Britain is divided between those who take a very negative view of the future of religion and, either explicitly or implicitly, defend the secularization thesis, and those who are rather more positive, believing that, albeit sometimes in different forms that institutional Christianity, religion is an integral feature of British society. For the former approach see Steve Bruce, *Religion in Modern Britain* (Oxford: Oxford University Press, 1995) and *God is Dead: Secularization in the West* (Oxford: Blackwell Publishers, 2002) along with Callum G. Brown, *The Death of Christian Britain: Understanding Secularization* (London: Routledge, 2002) and *Religion and Society in Twentieth-Century Britain* (Harlow: Pearson, 2006). For the latter approach see Grace Davie, *Religion in Britain since 1945: Believing without Belonging* (Oxford: Blackwell 1994) and Jane Garnett, Matthew Grimley, Alana Harris, William Whyte and Sarah Williams, eds., *Redefining Christian Britian: Post 1945 Perspectives* (London: SCM Press, 2006).

23 John M. Hull, *What Prevents Christian Adults from Learning?* (Valley Forge, PA: Trinity Press International, 1991), 22.

24 For the notion of 'habitus' see Edward Farley, *Theologia: The Fragmentation and Unity of Theological Education* (Philadelphia: Fortress Press, 1983), 35-39.

[25] Mark Gibbs and T. Ralph Morton, *God's Frozen People: A book for – and about – ordinary Christians?* (London: Collins Fontana Books, 1064).

[26] Although my theological outlook in many ways is somewhat different to that of P T Forsyth, I find my theological understanding of ministry remarkable similar, at least at the formal level, with that presented in his *Lectures on the Church and Sacraments* (London: Longmans, Green and Co., 1917). For an assessment of his views on ministry see David R. Peel, "P.T. Forsyth on Ministry: A Model for our Time?" in Alan P. F. Sell, ed., *P.T. Forsyth: Theologian for a New Millennium* (London: The United Reformed Church, 1999).

[27] See the Report of the 'Consultation of Eldership' held at the Royal Foundation of St. Katharine, London, October 24-26, 2006, available from The United Reformed Church.

RENEWING REFORMED THEOLOGY

The Word of God, the Bible and radical obedience

Lawrence Moore

"Where our understanding parts company with some is that our highest authority is God's Living Word, to be heard in and through the Bible, but which is not necessarily identical with the Bible."

The Word of God, the Bible and radical obedience...

Lawrence Moore

1. Reformata semper reformanda

"Reformed but always reforming"! At one level, this means nothing more than that the process of becoming more closely conformed to Jesus Christ is unfinished. Yet the United Reformed Church has, since its beginning, affirmed something far more radical: it has 'reserved its right to go on to make new statements of faith'. In other words, though a confessional Church in the sense that it regards the Apostles' and Nicene Creeds as expressing the essentials of the faith (both Catholic and Reformed), it does not regard itself as being confessionally *bound*. The truth of the faith it holds is not to be demonstrated by showing how it conforms to the articles of the Creed in a manner parallel to the way in which the United States Constitution operates, for example; rather, the Creeds are held ultimately to be *helpful* for as long as *they continue to express the faith as it is understood by the United Reformed Church.*

This is to walk an ecumenical tightrope. In terms of both its membership of the World Communion of Reformed Churches (WCRC) and its ecumenical partners, the United Reformed Church regards itself as being part of a *shared* faith tradition, and in large measure bound by it. We stand in continuity with this shared past: with the Apostles and the apostolic tradition; with the (predominantly western) Christian Church of the first fifteen centuries; with the Reformed tradition that we trace through Luther and Calvin, and then via the Presbyterian, Congregational and United Churches of Christ traditions.

To stand in continuity with tradition is to trace our pedigree; to say where we have come from. It is not to say that we *continue* in these traditions, or claim to be their contemporary representatives. In fact, we have said something different simply by coming into existence: we have said that we see ourselves and wish to be in a different place from any of our roots! And we have said that we desire to be in this new place because the old places were not good enough or faithful enough or relevant enough to the late 20th/early 21st centuries. They 'stated the faith and sought to make its implications clear'; in other words, they acted in obedience to the voice and call of God as they heard and understood it in their own times. We believe that God called the United Reformed Church into being in order to live out the answer to Jesus' high priestly prayer in John's gospel that "They may be one"[1].

God called us into being as a new expression of obedience. The 'final form' of our faith, or what discipleship means for us today, was not given either in the first four centuries or in the sixteenth. However formative those periods may have been, the United Reformed Church is saying more than that historical faith traditions must always take a form shaped by the contemporary context: it is saying that God might yet call us to something that may well be a radical departure from what we have always believed until now *because God is a still-speaking God*. We are committed, in other words, to *revelation continua* – a notion that many of our Reformed allies would find unacceptable. Yet we do so because our collective experience tells us that we can do no less. Our creeds and traditions have expressed and justified the reasons for how we have been in the past; the radically new obedience to which we have been called by God requires that we find ways of expressing and justifying that obedience. We have changed in the past in response to God's Word; we may have to change radically again because God is still speaking.

2. A Church of the Word

The possible necessity of having to change even the *Basis of Union* in response to God's call gives the distinctive shape and definition of how the United Reformed Church (like all Reformed churches) is a 'Church of the Word'. To give this classically Reformed emphasis to the Word is already an affirmation that God is a speaking God. Three things belong together in our particular understanding: a Living God, a Living Word and a Living Faith. This is expressed in *The Nature, Faith and Order of the United Reformed Church* as follows:

> "The highest authority for what we believe and do is God's Word in the Bible, *alive for his people today through the help of the Spirit*. We respond to *this* Word, whose servants we are with all God's people through the years."[2]

The Church is thus the Church according to the measure by which it is the community that is the living and lived expression of the Living Word that God speaks. Faith is understood as 'obedient response to God's Word'; that is something that the United Reformed Church shares with its WCRC partners. Where our understanding parts company with some is that our highest authority is God's *Living* Word, to be heard *in and through* the Bible, but which is not necessarily *identical* with the Bible. The Word 'whose servants we are' is the voice of the still-speaking God which we *hear* through the Bible but which is spoken *today* through the Holy Spirit.

Faithful obedience to the Word of God

Obedient conformity to the Word of God is thus different from asking 'What does the Bible say?' – ie from consulting the Bible as though it were a manual or encyclopaedia of God's thoughts and opinions and then simply 'doing what the Bible says'. Obedient conformity to the Word of God is reading the Bible in order to hear the

Word that the still-speaking God addresses to us through the Holy Spirit. God may *repeat* what is in the Bible; conversely, God may say something *different* from what is written in the Bible. The point is this: (1) The Bible is always the *medium through which* God, by the Holy Spirit, speaks a fresh Word to the Church and (2) Whether God repeats what the Bible says or says something different, that Word is always fresh and alive – God's Word for us today. We are servants of the still-speaking God – not servants of the Bible.

Of course, we have always recognised the need to interpret (rather than merely consult) the Bible. The same Word that God speaks in one age and context must be interpreted afresh in order to mean *the same thing* in a different context. We find this dynamic present within the Scriptures themselves: Yahweh is revealed in the Pentateuch as the God who was formerly worshipped as the Canaanite El deity, and *not* as the Ba'als. The Exile occasions a re-reading and re-appropriation of the earlier tradition in a radically altered context; the sacrificial system has similarly to be re-understood after the destruction of the Temple in 70 CE; the Gentile mission occasions a reinterpretation of Election and the later Pauline writings reinterpret eschatology in the face of the delayed Parousia. Most significantly, the designation of the Hebrew Scriptures as the 'Old Testament' is an affirmation and recognition that Jesus has both fulfilled and superseded the Law, and that God has done something radically new.

A new and different Word

The task of interpretation and reinterpretation is unavoidable in order to say anew what has been said in the past. What is distinctive about the United Reformed Church's way of being a 'Church of the Word' is that we assert – and practise – the notion that God might say something *different* from what is in the Bible (rather than saying the same thing is a new way). It is to move beyond the notion that 'God has spoken and what has been said is alive and relevant for today' in the conviction that God is *still* speaking and is sovereignly free to speak a *new* Word that is as authoritative as past words.

That we use the Bible in this way is evident from two key elements of our practice of ministry: from its inception, the United Reformed Church has ordained women and insisted that doubt about the validity of doing so disqualifies a potential candidate from ordination; secondly, the United Reformed Church has, since its inception, remarried and ordained divorcees. In both cases, the Church has a practice that runs counter to 'what the Bible says' while maintaining the authority of Scripture. How is this done with integrity?

We need to look carefully at what is said: "The highest authority for what we believe and do is God's Word in the Bible". Note that we do not say, "The highest authority... is the Bible". Nor do we say, "The highest authority... is God's Word, the Bible". We say, "The highest authority is God's Word... alive for his people today through the help of the Holy Spirit". *That* is the Word "whose servants we are". Where is that Word to be heard? Our unequivocal answer is, "in the Bible". That does not mean that we have only one 'conversation partner' – the Bible. God's Living Word is an *event*. There is the speaking God, the Bible, and the Holy Spirit. It is through the action and activity of the Spirit that the words of the Bible become for us the means by which God addresses the Church – itself the creation and locus of the Spirit's activity.

> In both cases, the Church has a practice that runs counter to 'what the Bible says' while maintaining the authority of Scripture. How is this done with integrity?

This is a distinctively Barthian move. God speaks – but God's Word is always mediated through the Bible. In this derivative sense, the Bible is properly called 'The Word of God' – not because it is *identical* with God's Word but because it is the indispensable instrument through which God *chooses* to speak via the Holy Spirit. There is one, unequivocal Word of God and that is Jesus Christ – the

Word made flesh – who is the subject of the Bible. Ultimately, it is because the Bible witnesses uniquely to *Jesus* that the Bible is, in this derivative sense, the Word of God. Or, as the United Reformed Church puts it, we hear "God's-Word-in-the-Bible". The authority of the Bible, in other words, is an authority *bestowed* upon it by God's choice of it as the means through which God still speaks.

There is no short cut to hearing God speak that bypasses the Bible. Nor will we accord the same ultimate authority to any Word of God heard other than through the Bible. Importantly, though, we accord ultimate authority to the Word of God heard *through* the Bible (and the agency of the Holy Spirit) and not *to* the Bible. Ultimate authority belongs not to God's Book but to God alone – the still-speaking God.

> There is no short cut to hearing God speak that bypasses the Bible.

A comma, not a full stop

God and God's Word are inseparable. Yet, as we have observed, that unequivocal identification of God and God's Word belongs properly only to The Word who became flesh rather than print. We quite properly retain a distinction between God and the Bible because we recognise the *way* in which God addresses us. The writer to the Hebrews puts it this way:

"Long ago, God spoke to our ancestors in many and various ways by the prophets, but in these last days he has spoken to us by a Son, whom he appointed heir of all things, through whom also he created the worlds. He is the reflection of God's glory and the exact imprint of God's very being." (Hebrews 1: 1-3a)

The Bible is a record of the God who discloses God's self to the community of faith. That disclosure happens over millennia and in all sorts of different contexts. It is a process. It develops. We may wish it were different, but it is not. The Bible was not dictated by God; it is the record of the faith of those who experienced God speaking. That faith grows, develops and changes as God continues to speak. The challenge of being God's people – the People of Yahweh and the Church – is continually to listen and to hear when God says something new (and possibly different) from the past. At that point, to appeal to the Scriptures and to say, "But God has spoken..." means that even those most deeply steeped in the biblical tradition can get God wrong.[3]

That means that we must, at times, distinguish between a) the being and character of God, on the one hand, and b) what the Bible says on the other. When we look at the debates over gender, race, and slavery, for instance, we should conclude this: it may indeed be the case that the Bible supports the inferiority of women to men and a male ministry, or the ideal of racial purity, or of slavery; the point is that even if the Bible does, the God *revealed* in the Bible does not! We only hear that Word with enough clarity, reassurance and compulsion to act on it *in spite of what the Bible says* when, through the Bible and the action of the Holy Spirit, we hear the voice of the still-speaking God.

3. God is still speaking — a vision for life

Vision4Life is the acknowledgement that we are in the process of learning to read and hear the Bible in this way. Our privileging of the historical-critical method has meant that we are schooled in 'biblical archaeology' – in learning to hear the written echoes of the ways in which God spoke *in* the past and *to* the past. We are 're-engaging with the Bible' in new ways of reading in order to hear the Living voice of the Living God to us – the living People of God. *Vision4Life* is a process of creating spaces in which God can address us freshly through the Bible. It is attuning ourselves to the voice of the Living, still-speaking God, in order to become more faithfully servants of the Living Word that God speaks.

The United Reformed Church is committed to living faithfully, rooted in the story of a Church that has come into being through God to be a witness to and agent of salvation in all times and in all places. It is self-consciously a 'rainbow Church' – a broad, inclusive community whose very life is intended as a witness to the fact that God has not abandoned the world to destruction but is in the process of saving it. The United Reformed Church is committed to living hopefully, convinced that it is *in via*. Who and what it is and will become is not determined by its roots and its past, but by its future as it listens for and responds in radical obedience to the Living Word spoken by the Living God who calls it to make a difference for Christ's sake.

References

1   John 17: 20-23. Cf article 9 of *The Basis of Union* and its expression in
    The Nature, Faith and Order of the United Reformed Church (Rejoice &
    Sing no. 761): 'We conduct our life together according to the Basis of
    Union in which we give expression to our faith in forms which we believe
    contain the essential elements of the Church's life, both catholic and
    reformed; but we affirm our right and readiness, if the need arises, to
    change the Basis of Union and *to make new statements of faith in ever*
    new obedience to the Living Christ' (italics mine). For '... the Living
    Christ', it would be possible – and more theologically correct – to
    substitute ' ... the still-speaking God'.

2   *Ibid* (italics mine).

3   Let me cite four examples: (1) the people of Judah who appealed to the
    Davidic covenant as counter to the prophetic warnings of impending
    exile were wrong. (2) When Job's friends appealed to Yahweh's ways in
    relation to suffering as understood by the tradition, they were wrong; (3)
    when Peter refused to believe that God was asking him to eat food
    previously declared unclean by Yahweh, he was wrong; (4) when Jesus
    was crucified as a blasphemer against God on the basis of the biblical
    tradition, the teachers of the Law were wrong about God. In each case,
    God was saying something new and different from what God had said in
    the past.

RENEWING REFORMED THEOLOGY
The Reformed Tradition and the Local Congregation

John Buchanan

"It is the post-denominational age.
People are simply not coming to our
churches because of the name."

The Reformed Tradition and the Local Congregation

John Buchanan

I discovered the Reformed Tradition long before I had a name for it. Martin Camroux's initial invitation, which surprised and flattered me, was to come to Cambridge and talk about "How a local congregation can discover the Reformed Tradition in a post-modern context when people increasingly sit light to tradition and denomination." Well – what self-respecting Presbyterian could resist an expansive topic like that?

Later, he condensed it to "Reformed Theology and the Local Congregation:" a little less fancy, but more manageable.

So that is what I will strive to do – talk about what I know best – the life of an American Presbyterian congregation, with a few brief forays into theology and the sociology of religion, for which I trust I can rely on your grace, with occasionally reference to the peculiarity of the religious situation in the United States, which reflects American author Phyllis Tickle's memorable image of an every-five-hundred year rummage sale – and occasionally feels like the ecclesiastical equivalent of a nuclear meltdown.[1]

In any event I fell in love with it before I had a name for it; in fact, before I could talk.

I became a Presbyterian, and thus an heir of the Reformed Tradition when the local Presbyterian pastor heard that a new young couple in the neighborhood – my parents – had a sick infant – that would be me – and paid a visit in their home. Apparently he prayed for me and they were so taken with his kindness that they started to attend his church, and one Sunday, presented me for baptism. I do not recall the occasion, but I know that he held me in his arms, poured the waters of baptism on my head, said my name, assured my parents of the covenantal promise of God, and told the congregation seated in the pews that morning, most, if not all of them long gone now, that they were my "sponsors," my Presbyterian Godparents, told them they were responsible for helping my parents to bring me up in the "nurture and admonition of the Lord" so that one day I would come, at last, to God's eternal kingdom.

> I loved the Reformed Tradition before I had a name for it. And even though it chose me, as it were, early on I began to chose it and claim it.

I am the pastor of a church that has a lot of young couples and consequently an abundance of babies. We celebrate the Sacrament of Baptism on the second Sunday of every month, and at the end of each baptism liturgy I invite the congregation to pray together:

> "Holy God, remind us of the promises given in our own baptism and renew our trust in you. Make us strong to obey your will, and to serve you with joy; for the sake of Jesus Christ our Lord. Amen."

And I do, every time, remember, and thank God for it. It took, that baptism did. I grew up in that congregation, and it was there that a seed was planted, and it was there that I began to ask the questions that led, drove, or dragged me to my vocation 25 years later.

I loved the Reformed Tradition before I had a name for it. And even though it chose me, as it were, early on I began to chose it and claim it.

There were plenty of times when I ignored it and it ignored me. My parents were not fervent Presbyterians. In fact, "fervent Presbyterian" is kind of an oxymoron. But going to church on Sunday was part of what we did. And

so it was sitting in our pew in that church that we sang –
it seems now – every week:

"Holy, Holy, Holy, Lord God Almighty
Early in the Morning, Our Song Shall Rise to Thee
Holy, Holy, Holy, Merciful and Mighty
God in Three Persons, blessed Trinity."

I had no idea what the second stanza was referring to
when we sang:

"All the saints adore thee
Casting down their golden crowns
Around the glassy sea"

but I loved the image, and through it all began to sense
something of the mystery and majesty of God.

One of our ministers, an eloquent and dramatic Texan
with a voice as rich and deep as an oil well – created a
Good Friday night candlelight service which raised
eyebrows: candles, after all, were the purview of our
Catholic neighbors; he read the accounts of the
crucifixion as the candles were gradually extinguished
and when in the darkness he cried out, "Eloi, Eloi, Lama
Sabacthani" I was touched to the quick with the suffering
and pathos.

It was the pastor who came when I was in High School
who sealed the deal. His name was Leslie Van Dine and
he was a decorated Army Sergeant in World War II, who
was wounded in battle and whose call to ministry came in
the midst of combat. He went to college after the war and
then to Yale Divinity School. I didn't know about Divinity
School, but I knew about Yale. He was scholarly,
undramatic, unlike his predecessor. He pretty much read
his sermon – but his sermons were laced with references
to books and plays and motion pictures. It never occurred
to me that ministers enjoyed motion pictures and plays.
He quoted *The New York Times*! My parents were
entranced. His Democratic politics irritated my

Republican father, but Dad couldn't help admire his literacy and his courage. His sermons were about life and I started to listen.

One time he said that he didn't expect people to agree with him, but he did hope they would respect him – and they did -and I became aware of a unique way of being Christian, which included a thoughtful engagement with the intellectual and political life of the world outside the doors of the church. I had not thought of that before. It certainly was a dramatic contrast with the way of being Christian taught at a large evangelical Baptist church I occasionally attended with chums – mainly because they sang lively songs, had food at every youth meeting and plentiful, attractive girls, none of which was true about my Presbyterian Church. But the Baptists were mainly concerned about my personal habits – smoking was sinful, so was drinking alcohol, thinking about sex was obviously bad – not to mention doing anything about it. Telling an adolescent boy not to think about sex is a little like trying to convince the sun not to rise (an unfortunate simile), even dancing was frowned on – and not a word about what was going on in the world.

What finally compelled me was my first encounter with science, Darwin and evolution. We didn't talk about it in my home, but I wasn't very old when I began to notice some problems with Biblical accounts of creation. For one thing, there are two of them, back to back and they don't agree on how things happened. In fact, they tell two fairly different stories. When I presented my observation to my Baptist chums they almost fainted. "It's true – it happened because the Bible is true, every word of it" they assured me.

So I took my new observations to Van Dine – who patiently explained that, yes, Presbyterians generally were not literalists, the Bible was true indeed, but the stories in the Bible were not always factually accurate. Evolution, many Presbyterians believe, is how it happened and it is not at all incompatible with what we believe about God.

Van Dine was also ecumenical. In our small city, he led the effort to organize a council of churches, a new idea at the time, bringing together Presbyterian, Methodist, Lutheran, Congregational churches. Rumour has it that one of his closest friends was a Rabbi with whom he enjoyed regular lunches.

He did not shy from controversy. This was a decade before the Civil Rights movement forever changed the church in the United States, but he frequently mentioned from the pulpit the injustice and racism rampant in American culture. One unforgettable incident still makes me smile. There is, or was – I haven't heard about them for years – an organization with a name in which you should have a particular interest: The Daughters of the American Revolution, the DAR. It was what the title indicated: an organization for women who could document their genealogical ties to the War for Independence – the end

> Telling an adolescent boy not to think about sex is a little like trying to convince the sun not to rise (an unfortunate simile), even dancing was frowned on — and not a word about what was going on in the world.

of which we celebrate on the 4th of July, an occasion my Scottish colleague, Calum MacLeod, tells me he observes as a day to "lament the lost colonies." The DAR was stuffy, snooty, elitist and very conservative politically. It was also openly racist. The DAR owned a popular auditorium in Washington called Constitution Hall, which it rented out for public concerts and lectures: Marian Anderson was a distinguished opera star who sang with all the best companies in the world. Her agent booked Constitution Hall for a recital. But when the DAR realized that an African-American, a black woman, would be singing on its stage, it cancelled the contract. It was in all the newspapers. Well – the Revd Van Dine decided to talk about it from the pulpit and he delivered an unforgettable line. He said the best part of the DAR is "underground." The congregation went silent. There were DAR members in the pews: my Aunts Peg and Inez were proud members. Some were outraged. My Dad thought it was the funniest thing he had ever heard. I felt proud.

So there it was: intellectual rigor, intentional worldliness, respect for other religious traditions, an open-minded trust in God; the Reformed Tradition given to me by a community of Presbyterian Christians and their pastors, who had promised years before, in my baptism, to nurture me and be my sponsors "to the end that I might confess Christ as my Lord."

My assignment did not include defining the Reformed Tradition. That has been done thoroughly and admirably already. But a few reflections will help me lead into the rest of my paper.

> Even in our more rigid and critical periods, Presbyterians have never claimed to be the only ones who will be saved or the 'one true church.'

Cynthia McCall Campbell, a good friend of mine, is the President of McCormick Theological Seminary in Chicago. The Reformed Tradition, Cynthia says, is "a way of thinking rather than a set of ideas, practices in commitments rather than specific doctrines."

Her list of "the habits of Reformed Practice" included:

Appreciation: "We honor and think we should know about the contributions of Christians of other eras, other cultures and other traditions. Even in our more rigid and critical periods, Presbyterians have never claimed to be the only ones who will be saved or the 'one true church.' We are ecumenical because we are Presbyterian."

An attitude of suspicion: "Presbyterianism has always argued that both church and Christian doctrine should always be in the process of being reformed. We are self-critical; a unique attitude these days." No one gets it all right all the time.

Engagement with the world: "the world is where we expect to meet God and see God at work."

Grace and Gratitude: "It is finally all about grace, about God's freely given love for the world told in the story of the Bible and made manifest in the life and ministry, death and resurrection of Jesus Christ." We can't earn it – we don't deserve it. All we can do is receive it gratefully and live it faithfully.[2]

Cynthia borrowed the phrase "Grace and Gratitude" from a distinguished British theologian who ended up in the United States, taught at the University of Chicago and Union Theological Seminary – Brian Gerrish. Obviously, he didn't invent it, but he has written about it elegantly. In *Saving and Secular Faith* Gerrish writes about our Presbyterian habit of writing new creeds or confessions of faith every generation or so. "Confessions of faith are reminders. Their primary use is not to smoke out heresy, but, primarily through constant recollection, to preserve identity. They prevent disintegration by maintaining a common language, a community of discourse, without which the fellowship would suffer group amnesia and might dissolve in a babble of discordant voices." Gerrish didn't intend it but he gave a pretty good description of the Presbyterian Church (USA).[3]

Gerrish says among the good and healthy aspects of Reformed Tradition is that it resists trivialization. He told about Robert Maynard Hutchins, one of the great names in American Higher Education and President of the University of Chicago. At first he regularly attended University Chapel until the day the Dean began his sermon: "Yesterday, I was on the golf course and as I teed off I was reminded that we must follow through in life."

Hutchins never attended another service. He explained: it wasn't as if what the Dean said was not true, but, he said, he had heard such truths sufficiently often and "sometimes in a better literary framework."[4]

For Brian Gerrish the Reformed Tradition is an attitude. He writes: "Keeping faith with the tradition, then, is not at all being bound by the letter of the law, it is more a matter of the company you keep, or the book you reach for first when you want to do your best thinking."[5]

Gerrish is particularly helpful when he talks about pluralism, an issue that may be the most important and difficult one for the church in the future: "To say that the Christian receives saving faith through the New Testament image of Jesus need not imply that faith cannot be had in any other way, or that no other religious traditions confer salvation. Hence it does not preclude or impede open and honest interfaith dialogue, but simply states the point from which, for the Christian, that dialogue begins."[6]

He does not mean a mushy reduction of Christianity to its least common denominator: "While genuine conversation is certainly inhibited by absolute and exclusive certainty, there cannot be a conversation at all if the Christian has nothing to say or no savior to confess . . . Christians will begin the dialogue convinced that what has been given to them through Jesus Christ is for all humanity. But Jesus Christ may not be humanity's sole access to it. There is no way to know that in advance, before one has listened to the other parties in the conversation." [7]

One more voice: Nicholas Wolterstorff, who teaches Philosophy at Yale University and is a Reformed Christian:

"God's call to those who are Christ's followers is to participate in the life of the church and to think, feel, speak and act as Christians within the institutions and practices that we share with our fellow human beings. We are not called to go off by ourselves somewhere to set up our own economic practices, our own political institutions, our own art world, our own world of scholarship: we are called to participate within our own shared human practices and institutions"[8]

Inching ever closer to the topic you invited me to address, a few words about "the current religious situation in the United States."

In *The Great Emergence* Phyllis Tickle likens what is happening to us to an "every-five hundred-year rummage sale." (Do you have rummage sales in Great Britain? Dreadful affairs where people bring stuff they no longer want to the church, school, fire hall – whoever is sponsoring it – where it is sorted, priced, put on display and other people come and buy it.) Rummage Sale means getting rid of whatever has outlived its usefulness and beginning again, leaner, smaller and more nimble.

> ...my church, the Presbyterian Church (USA), has essentially lost half its membership from the 1960s to today

Tickle says something like that happens every 500 years – all the way back to the Exodus and Davidic monarchy, Exile, the early Christian Church; 500 years later the Fall of Rome and Gregory the Great; 500 years later the Great Schism; 500 years later Reformation; and now – this – whatever history will call it.

Two things happen with each successive Rummage Sale: the old institution gets smaller and better, and a new institution is born and both of them march into the future, each of them stronger, more nimble, responsive and faithful, than before.[9]

I devoutly hope she is right. At the moment the mainline churches in the United States are all in the process of steady numerical decline and have been for forty years, with a consequent loss in position and influence in American culture.

Not to belabor the point, but my church, the Presbyterian Church (USA), has essentially lost half its membership from the 1960s to today: from close to 4 million to slightly more than 2 million. Something similar is occurring in every part of the family of Mainline, or Mainstream Churches: United Church of Christ, Methodist, Episcopal, American Baptist (progressive), Disciples of Christ, Lutherans – not quite as dramatic but still down. Conservative Evangelical churches at the same time, have done relatively well, led by the Southern Baptists, but even their growth seems to have stalled. Within each denomination, a culture war rages between progressives (liberals) and conservatives and the flash point for decades had been sexuality, and the matter of ordination of gay and lesbian persons. Some denominations have seen small schisms – the Episcopalian and Lutheran for instance.

> Within each denomination, a culture war rages between progressives (liberals) and conservatives and the flash point for decades had been sexuality

At the same time Mega-churches appeared: huge, independent congregations, ordinarily built around the personality and charisma of the organizing pastor. They are intentionally non-denominational – undenominational is more accurate – and they have eliminated the trappings, paraphernalia, liturgies and even the furniture of traditional religion. There are auditoriums rather than sanctuaries, theatre seats rather than pews, stage instead of chancel, songs instead of hymns – projected on a pull-down screen rather than hymnal, a praise band rather than pipe organ, a stool, or hand-held mike instead of pulpit, and a "message" rather than a sermon. Some are quite good at what they do and faithful in their presentation of the gospel and its missional implications. Some are banal, trivial and so focused on meeting the needs of needy worshippers that the gospel – incarnation, discipleship, service, justice, giving life away – is simply not evident anywhere. There are no crosses.

There is little evidence that people are abandoning mainline churches to join mega-churches. But there is plenty of evidence that the mega-churches, with their determinedly anti-traditional church ethos, attract folk who dropped out of church a long time ago.

Church historian Martin Marty studies and writes about what is happening, helpfully. In *The Protestant Voice in American Pluralism* he describes how the Colonial "Big Three," Anglican, Presbyterian and Congregational thoroughly dominated during colonial, revolution and post revolution American. There were few Roman Catholics, fewer Jews and no one had ever seen a Muslim.[10] Pluralism is what happened, slowly at first, but rapidly after immigration laws were loosened in the 1960s. Cities – where mainline churches declined, suburbs emerged and burgeoned and the old mainline churches were simply not nimble enough, or creative enough, to respond.

It is the post-denominational age. People are simply not coming to our churches because of the name. They used to. Presbyterians would drive by half a dozen Methodist, United Church of Christ, Baptist churches to find their way to First Presbyterian, but not much any longer. Other features attract: opportunities for youth ministry, music and the arts, quality of worship and preaching, mission, and parking. All the church growth experts say that adequate parking is the one indispensible requirement for a viable 21st century church. We, by the way, have no parking at all at the Fourth Presbyterian Church of Chicago.

About our loss of position in American culture. Douglas John Hall, a Reformed, Canadian theologian, says it's a good thing. We used to dominate. Most Senators, Congressional Representatives – were members of mainline churches. When the media wanted a religious spokesperson to comment on this or that public issue, they called on the national offices of the Presbyterians or Episcopalians. The Stated Clerk of the Presbyterian Church was a man of such prestige that he, Eugene Carson Blake, appeared on the cover of *TIME* magazine in the 1950s. That would be unthinkable today. It has been decades since anyone inquired as to how we Presbyterians thought about anything, although we keep soldiering on, expressing our opinions on everything whether anyone is listening or not.

Hall says the mainline churches, particularly the Colonial Big Three, were virtually the "established church" in a culture that was consciously Christian – Christendom, that is to say. It is gone, utterly, absolutely gone. As a cultural, political and social phenomenon, Christendom is dead and there is now an opportunity for the churches to renew themselves and live faithfully. [11]

In the midst of all of that, all that social complexity and cultural upheaval (and I haven't even mentioned the culture war raging in the United States between progressives and conservatives and which has emerged within churches) general decline of mainline churches, and the advent of a new secularism – there is an anomaly – churches that keep their names and traditions, theologically, liturgically, missionally – do quite well. Some are in the suburbs. Some are in the center of the city. I am privileged to be the Pastor of one of them – the Fourth Presbyterian Church of Chicago. Fourth was the name chosen in the 1870s, when two smaller congregations merged, and since there was a first, second, third, fifth, sixth and seventh, but for some odd reason no fourth, that is the name the new church proudly claimed for itself. No one ever accused Presbyterians of being overly imaginative.

My conclusion, after 25 years, is that people are attracted to Fourth Presbyterian Church because of the Reformed Tradition, although they would not have a name for it, even as I didn't when it began to compel me.

A word about the congregation. The church building is located on Michigan Avenue, the main, high-end retail shopping thoroughfare in the city and one of the most expensive and profitable avenues in the world. When the church was built in 1912-1914, none of that was true. In fact, the site was on an unpaved road, with the shore of Lake Michigan just a few hundred feet away. The building is neo-Gothic, one of the best examples of the work of Ralph Adams Cram, the premier Gothic architect of the day in the United States – whose work included Princeton University and the Cathedral of St. John the Divine in New York City.

Our building is a gem, a sanctuary that seats 1400, now surrounded by tall, residential high rises. The John Hancock Building – 100 stories, is directly across the street. Our neighbors include vertical shopping malls and high end hotels, The Four Seasons and Ritz Carlton. Because of the high rises, the residential population around the church is large – and growing. A little more than a mile to the west a Public Housing Project is in the process of transition. For fifty years Cabrini Green became the worst of our experiment in high rise public housing, a decaying concentration of poverty, unemployment, dysfunctional families, and crime. Both – the conspicuous affluence and commercialism of our immediate environment and the proximity of our neighbors in Cabrini Green have, for decades, defined the church's life and outreach.

> As a cultural, political and social phenomenon, Christendom is dead and there is now an opportunity for the churches to renew themselves and live faithfully.

The congregation has grown steadily in the past 25 years, from 2400 to 6200. It is a diverse congregation: there are more young single and young married than most churches, with lots of children and young people – many, many more than the designers ever anticipated would be there. There are business executives, doctors and attorneys and there are school teachers, nurses, and marginally employed, socially marginalized, and homeless people. The congregation is mostly white, but there are growing numbers of African Americans, Latinos and Asians.

Our three morning worship services, 8:00, 9:30, 11:00 am (9:30 and 11:00 with full sanctuary) are traditional. Clergy wear robes, Geneva tabs, and clerical collars. The liturgy is Reformed – praise and adoration, the Word read and preached, prayers of the people, offering, blessing. Traditional hymns are sung, and the church has a long tradition of excellent music, with a large pipe organ, professional singers in the choir and a brass ensemble that plays for worship once a month.

The music is good. People know what to expect and love it. No one has ever suggested we hire a praise band.

The music is varied: from classics to contemporary compositions and spirituals. A 4:30 pm service uses jazz as the musical idiom and is attracting new and curious people.

> Karl Barth was right when he said a Christian must have an open Bible in one hand and a newspaper in the other.

My preaching is guided by the lectionary – but not chained to it. For instance, this autumn, in response to the new atheism and the rash of best sellers in the U.S., making the case for atheism, Christopher Hitchens, *God is Not Great*, and Richard Dawkins, *The God Delusion*, I am preaching a series of sermons on "What the Bible Says and What We Believe about God." There is nothing more tedious than a preacher talking about his or her own preaching, so I will resist the temptation except to say I read a lot and work hard at it and strive to be faithful to scripture and relevant to what is happening in my city, nation and world. References to the economy, war in Afghanistan, the atrocious epidemic of guns and consequent deaths of children in Chicago, find their way into sermons. I try not to be partisan politically. Some people tell me I am not successful. I simply insist that what is going on outside is important inside the church, and that Karl Barth was right when he said a Christian must have an open Bible in one hand and a newspaper in the other.

We value the Reformed emphasis on the life of the mind. An Academy of Faith and Life is the name for our Adult Education program, consisting of one ongoing adult Bible Study class – and literally dozens of short term classes and one-time lectures on topics as varied as The Theology of John Calvin, The Parables, Religion in Film and Art, and Islam. Several hundred people participate in one or more of these activities annually. We also hold weekly Sunday School for several hundred youngsters, a Confirmation Class of forty 8th graders this year and Junior and Senior High youth programs for study, fellowship and service and mission trips.

We strive to be ecumenical and respectful of other faith traditions.

One of the first things I did when arriving 25 years ago was call on the local Roman Catholic Archbishop, Joseph Cardinal Bernadin, and invite him to preach at Fourth Presbyterian Church. He was delighted and did it – twice – and so has his successor Francis Cardinal George. That, and community Thanksgiving Services with Holy Name Cathedral and the local Jewish synagogue provided the framework for Interfaith services at the time of the September 11, 2001 attacks on the World Trade Center.

Our relationship with Chicago Sinai Congregation bears mentioning. When an older synagogue decided to relocate in our neighborhood and build a new building, the Rabbi asked to see me to talk about an idea he and his leaders had. Synagogues are built to accommodate the crowds for the High Holy Days – which customarily are huge, many times larger than regular Sabbath services. So, Rabbi Berman asked, would we consider allowing Congregation Sinai to use our sanctuary for Rosh Hashanah and Yom Kippur services, which would allow them to build a synagogue more appropriate for the numbers of people who attend Sabbath services.

I wish I could tell you that our leaders responded immediately and positively. Actually, something better happened. We had a good, strong conversation about the meaning of our worship space, whether it was sacred and exactly what we meant by that, and about our Jewish neighbors, how our faith in Jesus Christ informed our stance toward theirs. Were they targets for evangelization or something more complicated than that?

Happily, we resolved the question by issuing an invitation for High Holy Day observances to be scheduled in our sanctuary. And that is what has been happening for 10 years. Every September/October on several mornings, afternoons and evenings, our building is filled, standing room only, with our Jewish neighbors who are now so accustomed to the arrangement that many of their members have staked out their favorite Presbyterian pew – just as my own people do.

It has been an altogether happy relationship – with several joint adult education seminars, and joint service projects. And it has been a symbol of something deeper and more important – a theological tradition that is open and respectful. People know about it, are grateful for it, and are compelled by it.

The events of 9/11 changed a lot in my country and culture and church. For one thing no one knew a thing about Islam. I managed to get through four years of undergraduate and four years of graduate education without Islam being mentioned other than very peripherally. Nearly a quarter of the world's population is Muslim, but my education barely acknowledged the fact. Now – people were attacking us, calling out as they crashed airplanes into skyscrapers, "Allah Akbar" – God is Great. The reaction in my country was immediate and harsh. Supported by many in the media Americans concluded that Islam had attacked us: Islam which we now believed as a violent, hateful religion. The media was full of it. The Internet made it worse. It still festers.

So we invited Islamic scholars to come and teach in our Academy for Faith and Life. I taught an early morning course on *The Battle for God*, Karen Armstrong's superb study of Islam. We invited the Council of Islamic Organizations to send a representative to read from the Koran in our community Thanksgiving Service, and we invited Muslim groups to join us for discussion, service projects and fellowship – all of which is happening. We're not only learning that Islam is not an essentially violent religion and feeling good about it: we are, I believe, expressing our theological tradition in a way that provides people with an alternative notion of what it means to be a Christian church in a pluralistic culture.

Recently, as the 9th anniversary of 9/11 approached, and as the culture war raged and deepened, anti-Islamic rhetoric increased and evolved into Islamophobia. An eccentric leader of a tiny organization in Gainesville, Florida, Dove World Outreach Center – I refuse to call it a church – announced that he and his followers would observe the 9th anniversary of 9/11 by burning copies of the Koran on Saturday, September 11. I'm not sure if you even heard about it, but literally everyone on the United States did. CNN and al Jazeera picked it up and quickly reaction in the Muslim world became predictably aggressive. General David Petraeus, Commander of NATO forces in Afghanistan, personally called Terry Jones and told him that what he threatened to do was causing NATO, American and Afghan civilian casualties.

> We invited the Council of Islamic Organizations to send a representative to read from the Koran in our community Thanksgiving Service

At our staff meeting that week, it was clear that it was an important moment and an opportunity to express who we are – contrary to the despicable image of Christianity expressed by Terry Jones. So we telephoned our friends at the Downtown Islamic Center and asked if we could be helpful. The Director explained that Eid, the last day of Ramadan, which Muslims observe with celebration and picnics, was going to fall on September 11th this year and he and all Muslims were afraid that the media would portray their Eid observance as a celebration of what happened on 9/11/01. Would we come and be present with them? So we hurriedly got a statement of support out to our Session – thanks to the marvel of email, and one of our ministers and a few members attended the Eid observance and read the statement. It was, I am told, helpful and a powerful experience.

The statement and the sermon I preached the next day are available. I told the congregation about what we had done to reach out in support of Muslim neighbors and in order to express our respect, our revulsion at the threat to burn the Koran, and our shame that somehow this was being portrayed as a Christian response to Islam I decided to read from the Koran in worship. Our people were deeply moved. It was, I hope and believe, a genuine expression of a theological tradition that is open, inclusive and respectful.

Finally our tradition shapes our missional responsibilities and outreach in the world. Within the umbrella of the Session there are nine outreach programs, each headed by a Director and with staff support.

A **Counseling Center** which provides therapeutic services on a sliding fee scale to members and non-members. The Director is a PhD Psychologist and his staff includes 11 other therapists.

A **Center for Life and Learning** that focuses on the aging population and provides programs, field trips, seminars and special activities.

A **Center for Whole Health**, led by a Registered Nurse offers basic health education seminars, screenings, referrals, and basic care to members and neighbors.

A **Magnet School Program** collaborates with three urban elementary schools to support teachers, provide supplemental materials and provides music and dance programs for urban youngsters throughout the academic year in their schools and in a special summer program at the church.

A **Preschool** offers a program for 2, 3, and 4 year-old pre-kindergarten children and their families.

A **tutoring program**, our largest outreach program by far, brings together 400 urban youngsters for an hour and a half with a volunteer Tutor weekly to help with school work, social skills, and to be a caring adult presence with our most vulnerable city children.

As it turns out – our tutoring program is our most effective evangelism enterprise. Half of the tutors are non-members. Typically they are young, new to the city, employed in business, the law, health care and want to make a difference. They meet their youngsters in the church building – maybe they haven't been in a church for years and at some point they make a connection between the child they have come to love and the big church that is making all this happen and the next thing you know they have attended a new member class and are standing in front of us, or kneeling for baptism and promising to be Christ's faithful disciple.

Beyond these programs, that are administered by a non-profit corporation we have formed, which allows the programs to receive corporate and public funding, we have a scholarship program to assist promising public school students. An advocacy program which allows members an opportunity to join with other members in expressing their voice on issues of public significance; and a Mission Trip program open to members who wish to travel, to learn and serve and build houses and schools in Cuba, Honduras, Guatemala, Kenya, Mozambique, Cameroon, Colombia, Native American reservations, and New Orleans, still emerging from the devastation of Hurricane Katrina.

I think I have evidence that when the best of Reformed Tradition is expressed in the life of a congregation, when the theological tradition shapes the life of the church – the result is interesting, lively and compelling.

Brian Gerrish writes:

> "A confessional tradition is more than its creeds and confessions of faith: it includes hymns and histories, the biographies of heroes and treatises of theologians, reports and pronouncements of church assemblies, inherited forms of worship and polity, and – along with everything else – an intangible ethos that is easier to describe than to define" (p. 84).

It may not always be successful – if our only way of describing success is in terms of numbers – size of membership, number of people in worship, dollars in the budget. At my ordination, the minister at the time of the church that gave me the Reformed Tradition delivered the charge to the pastor. I have forgotten almost every word spoken on that occasion 47 years ago, and there were a lot of them. But I remember this:

> "John," he said, looking directly at me, "God has called you, not to be successful, but to be faithful."

But when it/the Reformed Tradition is expressed genuinely as one way of following the Lord Jesus Christ in the life of the church, his Body on Earth, and in the world he loved – it will be a community of people – interesting, lively, authentic and joyful.

References

1   Phyllis Tickle, *The Great Emergence* (Grand Rapids, MI: Baker Books, 2008)

2   Cynthia M. Campbell, Convocation Address (Chicago, IL: McCormick Theological Seminary, August 31, 2004).

3   Brian A. Gerrish, *Saving and Secular Faith, An Invitation to Systematic Theology* (Minneapolis, MN: Fortress/Augsburg Press, 1999) 56.

4   *Ibid.*, p. 75-76.

5   *Ibid.* p. 84.

6   *Ibid.* p. 101.

7   *Ibid.* p. 102.

8   Nicholas Wolterstorff, *The Way to Justice, How My Mind Has Changed* (Chicago, IL: *The Christian Century*, 12/1/09) 26-30.

9   *op cit.* (Tickle)

10   Martin E. Marty, *The Protestant Voice in American Pluralism* (Athens, GA: University of Georgia Press, 2004).

11   Douglas John Hall, *The End of Christendom and the Beginning of Christianity* (Harrisburg, PA: Wipf and Stock, 2002)

A UNITED REFORMED CHURCH PUBLICATION

RENEWING REFORMED THEOLOGY
Christian
Confidence

Roberta Rominger

"It is the post-denominational age.
People are simply not coming to our
churches because of the name. They
used to."

Christian Confidence

Roberta Rominger

It was 2002 that we received the results at a very memorable meeting of the URC Mission Council. My memory of that October morning paints the presentation in a truly dismal light. We knew that our age profile peaked in the 65 to 74-year-old range. We knew that women outnumbered men in our churches two to one. We knew that our coffee mornings were better attended than our Bible study groups, and it was no great surprise that the vast majority of our members were long-time attenders rather than newcomers. But what I distinctly remember is a slide which doesn't appear in the set downloadable from the URC website, so I hope I'm not making this up. The question was something like, How important is God in your life? A) Absolutely centrally important; B) Fairly important; C) Not terribly important; D) God is not important to me. All the Baptists, we were told, had ticked A. URC members had mostly gone for B. God is fairly important in my life. I wanted to crawl under my chair. It was that, coupled with an equally grim finance report, which led Mission Council to send the General Secretary away to conduct an urgent and radical review of the life of our church, what became known as Catch the Vision.

Although Catch the Vision would be remembered primarily for structural and financial reform, its steering group noted from the beginning that our malaise was spiritual and theological. We had lost the plot somewhere along the line. Our strong convictions regarding global economic justice and community service were not matched by strong convictions about the content of our faith. The invitation to think of ourselves as "God's people, transformed by the gospel, making a difference to the world's kingdoms for the sake of Christ's Kingdom" still hangs before us like a golden vision in the face of the shabbiness we see when we look in the mirror.

This morning I would like to explore the question of Christian confidence. On the surface that is a sociological question, or maybe a psychological one, but I would submit that it is also theological. What are we thinking about God and the Christian story that leaves us so tongue-tied and unsure? How do we understand the reluctance so many of us feel to articulate our faith at all? How do we find our way to a sense of theological exploration and adventure at the centre of local church life, instead of the reticence and avoidance that we suffer in so many places?

On the surface it is easy to diagnose the problem. A church that has been in decline for as long as anyone can remember is hardly going to be confident. Decline certainly hits the confidence of those in leadership in our churches. When you've prayed your hardest and given your best and tried everything you know with all the sacrifice you can muster, and nothing ever seems to "work", it is hardly surprising that you doubt both yourself and your faith. In the opening chapter of *Reforming Theology*, David Peel points to other explanations, three of them. Theology as a discipline has become associated with the preparation of people for ordained ministry, like medicine for doctors. Poor old Schleiermacher has something to answer for here as he fought for the place of theology in the secular universities so that ministers would be trained alongside lawyers and doctors. If theology is for experts, it's not for the likes of the people in the pews. They can safely leave it to their ministers the way they leave the workings of their car engines to auto

> When you've prayed your hardest and given your best and tried everything you know with all the sacrifice you can muster, and nothing ever seems to "work", it is hardly surprising that you doubt both yourself and your faith.

mechanics. I don't really want to understand how my car engine functions. I just want it to work. Happy to leave theology to the experts too. David then points to the carving up of theology into a variety of disciplines – systematic theology vs. practical theology and so forth – each with its own methodology and literature. If even the experts don't navigate comfortably across the breadth of theological discourse, why should an ordinary mortal even presume to try? The third disincentive has to do with the tools themselves. We borrow freely from secular and academic toolboxes and none of us would go back to the days before historical criticism or literary theory or even counselling training, but an ordinary person confronted with a passage from scripture or even a neighbour in pain is now likely to feel inadequate on account of not possessing the proper tools. I cannot see that the solution lies in academic theology. Not in the first instance, anyway. A reinvigorated Reformed theology could indeed renew and enliven the church, and with that renewal and life would come confidence, but first we need theologically hungry people. Before the intellectual adventure can get underway, we need people who are wondering about things. Where are questions born? And how do you enable people to be confident enough to ask them? How did it happen for any of us?

I propose that we need to address a taboo subject, namely our experience of God, personal and corporate. I believe that Christian confidence comes from knowing God's hand on our lives. This is a matter of experience, of personal story, before it is a matter of cognitive enquiry. I really don't see any substitute for that. No matter how shiny our ideas, how clever our arguments, how devastating our critiques, unless we know ourselves claimed by God and empowered by God for God's purposes, full (if unlikely) participants in a vibrant tradition stretching back to Christ himself, we will always be undermined by feelings of inadequacy. Scratch the surface and you'll always find the assumption that real church isn't what we've got here, it happens someplace else. Or, that there was a golden age and it's past and we are just pathetic and unworthy inheritors going through the motions.

I offer this because when I look around the United Reformed Church I actually see a church that deserves to feel confident – at least, a lot more confident than it ever seems to feel. Any of you who were at General Assembly in July will remember the electricity in the air during the presentation of the community awards. Normally that competition gets five or six applications and three prizes are awarded. This year there were 82 applications and five awards and I believe the judges when they say they struggled to limit it to five. What imaginative, brave, committed work: this was no dying church we were looking at. And the Children's Assembly, true excellence in children's work. Those children genuinely contributed to the work of Assembly – where else in the Christian world does that happen? And last December's multicultural celebration in Birmingham – what a foretaste of the Kingdom! The theology I would like to recover for the URC is an unapologetic celebration that God is around and God is using us, the love of Christ is finding expression in things we do and lives are being transformed. We're not pseudo Christians praying that nobody finds us out, we are the Body of Christ. This is it. We're not off the map, we're on it. God is willing to do business with us. But because of our inability to own and claim personal and corporate experience of a living, immanent God, we cower around apologetically instead of standing tall and presenting ourselves as disciples of Jesus Christ. The Roman Catholic theologian, James Alison, has a model for our engagement with God that offers helpful insights both into our lack of confidence and how we might begin to turn it around. Alison speaks of God as the "Other other". He says that the great discovery of the Hebrew people was not that there was one God as opposed to many gods but that the one God had nothing whatever in common with the many gods, the tribal gods or nature gods their neighbours worshipped.

The one God was of a whole different order of being. Their God was a "complete turning inside out of any religious understanding available in any culture..."[1]

In a bizarre image, but one that I find really helpful, Alison explains this turning inside out. He invites us to imagine buying sausage rolls in a local baker's and carrying them away in a brown paper bag. If you're a vegetarian like me I'm sure it's acceptable to substitute a lovely croissant. You eat the pastry and what's left is crumbs in the bottom of the bag. "Now," Alison writes, "imagine that this bag is upside down, so that the open bit is at the bottom, and the closed bit is at the top. Let us imagine that since this is a pretty classy bakery, there are all sorts of quality crumbs, of an energetic nature, and these crumbs are clustering inside the top of the bag, pushing and shoving the edge of the bag, trying to stretch its limits, trying to see out through the bag, which they can a little, since a brown paper bag *is* slightly see-through, and yet lends a mistakenly sepia tint to everything you see through it. Well, of course, the more the crumbs push and pull, all they do is push and pull the bag more firmly around them, and everything they see is in fact a function of the bag and its being pushed and pulled around by them."[2] God, he says, is a big fist coming down from outside who turns the paper bag inside out. At first the crumbs do not notice. They are still trying for all they're worth to see through the brown paper to the mystery on the other side. And then one of them realises. Look! This mystery we've been trying to penetrate, it's all around us. It is utterly Other than what we are. We are not equipped to comprehend it. But if we can acknowledge the inadequacy of our five senses and allow our intuition and imagination to challenge our reason and enlarge the picture for us, the adventure begins.

> Look! This mystery we've been trying to penetrate, it's all around us. It is utterly Other than what we are.

God would be unknowable to us except that God so desires to be known. God uses any and every means of revealing Godself to us. That's a human intuition to be found across cultures and religions. We become Christian at the point when we say that the supreme revelation of that amazing reality is the life and death and rising of Jesus Christ. So Christian confidence begins with the experience of awakening of a crumb. Here are three awakening stories to lay on the table for our examination.

Presbyterian theologian Frederick Buechner is well known as someone who urges the rest of us to listen to our lives so as to discern signs of God. In his later years much of his writing has been to search out the meaning of his father's suicide which happened when he was a small boy. But in a more day-to-day example he offers this:

> I remember sitting parked by the roadside once, terribly depressed and afraid about my daughter's illness and what was going on in our family, when out of nowhere a car came along down the highway with a license plate that bore on it the one word out of all the words in the dictionary that I needed most to see exactly then. The word was TRUST. What do you call a moment like that? Something to laugh off as the kind of joke life plays on us every once in a while? The word of God? I am willing to believe that maybe it was something of both, but for me it was an epiphany. The owner of the car turned out to be, as I'd suspected, a trust officer in a bank, and not long ago, having read an account I wrote of the incident somewhere, he found out where I lived and one afternoon brought me the license plate itself, which sits propped up on a bookshelf in my house to this day. It is rusty around the edges and a little battered, and it is also as holy a relic as I have ever seen.[3]

We become Christian at the point when we say that the supreme revelation of that amazing reality is the life and death and rising of Jesus Christ.

A similar experience from a member of the United Reformed Church. At a recent URC event a young woman got up during worship to give a testimony. She spoke of the downward spiral her life had taken over the course of the last year to a point where, in utter desolation, she found herself kneeling in the rain in a hospital car park. She prayed: God, if you're there, you need to do something now, because if you don't, I'm not going to make it. And then she looked up and there in the sky was a rainbow. A double rainbow, to be precise. It saved her life. There she was standing before us, vulnerable but confident.

Another story, from Barbara Brown Taylor, an American, an Episcopal priest, from her book, *An Altar in the World.*

I did not have a single clue what I would do when I graduated [from theological seminary]... So I began asking God to tell me what I was supposed to do. What was my designated purpose on this earth? How could I discover the vocation that had my name on it? Since this was an important prayer, I searched for the right place to pray it. After a few lacklustre attempts by the side of my bed and a few more in various cubbyholes around campus, I found a fire escape that hung precariously from the side of a deserted Victorian mansion next door to the Divinity School. That same night I crept over there after dark. Stepping over the "Danger: Keep Off" sign at the bottom, I climbed to the top, listening to the bolts creak as I tried to minimize the thundering of my feet on the narrow iron steps. I was so reluctant to take my hands off the rails that layers of old paint crackled under my palms like cornflakes. At the top I had to take a deep breath before I could let go of my handholds long enough to turn around. I did it as fast as a trapeze artist, gripping the rails again as soon as I sat down.

The fire escape turned out to be an excellent place to pray. Doing something that scared me cranked up my courage. Escaping up instead of down prepared me for other reversals. There was not a chance anyone could sneak up on me. The wind smelled like the moon. I went up there so many times in the weeks that followed that I no longer remember which night it was that God finally answered my prayer. I do not think it was right at the beginning, when I was still saying my prayers in words. I think it came later, when I had graduated to inchoate sounds. Up on that fire escape, I learned to pray the way a wolf howls. I learned to pray the way that Ella Fitzgerald sang scat.

Then one night when my whole heart was open to hearing from God what I was supposed to do with my life, God said, "Anything that pleases you." "What?" I said, resorting to words again. "What kind of an answer is that?"

"Do anything that pleases you," the voice in my head said again, "and belong to me."[4]

Three stories. An unholy mess or the stirrings of revelation? As I understand it, the Reformed tradition overall is wary of this sort of witness for a whole list of reasons. Subjectivity! Very dangerous. If the four primary sources for Christian theology are scripture, reason, tradition and experience, clearly scripture comes at the top of the list and experience so far to the bottom that in some versions of the list it doesn't appear at all. We take seriously the sinfulness of human nature. Who among us can possibly be trusted to intuit the ways of God, prone as we are to self-centredness and self-deception, rationalisation and wishful thinking? A faith that sets each of us up as some kind of authority is a nonsense of a faith, an exercise in sheer chaos.

And of course, it doesn't even take sinfulness to make personal revelations problematic. We're limited. We're fallible. We're all beginners when it comes to faith. We don't know what we're doing. You and I would have other reservations to add to the list. Personal experience is a bit of a cultural bandwagon just now. The only thing I am to take more seriously than my own experience is the experience of some celebrity. Surely as Christian disciples we cannot let ourselves be swayed uncritically by trends of the day. What hope is there for a society that honours personal experience and distrusts inherited wisdom? Where in the world are we if each person gets to be his or her own personal, individual authority? Where my truth is as good as your truth and it is in terribly bad taste for you to try to impose your truth on me? The Pope is not impressed by this and I'm sure we're not either. I feel the heavy burden of proof lying on my shoulders as I propose personal experience as the route to confidence.

But I am aware that there have also been times and places in the Reformed tradition where testimony has been a significant element in worship. It continues to be so among the Ghanaian members of the church where I worship. Our minister has invited people to come up and tell their stories and we've sung praises to God with them and prayed with them. (Granted, some of them are Methodists!)

> What hope is there for a society that honours personal experience and distrusts inherited wisdom?

Surely the respect for testimony is only just beneath the surface in the Basis of Union, where it says that the Word of God in the Old and New Testaments, discerned under the guidance of the Holy Spirit, is the supreme authority for our faith and conduct. How is the Holy Spirit to guide except by those flashes of insight that one person shares with the rest, and the shivers of recognition that run up our spines as confirmation? And what *are* we doing in Church Meeting if it isn't testing some inspiration to judge whether it is what God is calling us to be or do together?

Sticking with what we've been taught or what our reason tells us and ignoring what could be the voice of God speaking into our separate lives and our lives as churches is not an option if we are to be faithful to our tradition. A church that claims as its identity 'reformata semper reformanda' needs to think seriously about how it expects ongoing reformation to happen. The witness of scripture is that the Spirit comes to somebody with a crazy vision that turns out to be the next giant step for the whole people. Think of Abraham and his covenant, Moses and his burning bush, Isaiah and the promise of home. Incarnation was not expected. Nor resurrection. Nor Pentecost. And even the early Christian community that had the Christ event for reference stumbled over Peter and Cornelius, the outrageous notion that the gospel was for unclean Gentiles as much as for them. James Alison's picture of the crumbs hanging onto their paper bag looking out into the immensity of a world utterly beyond them is exactly what it feels like.

But our tradition gives us resources for seeing and thinking and judging. We are a community that immerses itself in scripture. We take it very seriously as a window into the ways of God. We ponder it and offer ourselves to be shaped by it so that, by the grace of God, we are able to recognise the movement of the Spirit in our lives, in our life together, when it happens. We attend Church Meeting and engage in that corporate work of discernment over matters large and small. And make

...make no mistake: our salvation hinges on the little things as much as the big ones, the petty power struggles we fall into as well as the great acts of courage we sometimes find ourselves called to.

no mistake: our salvation hinges on the little things as much as the big ones, the petty power struggles we fall into as well as the great acts of courage we sometimes find ourselves called to. I believe that much of the United Reformed Church's failure of confidence is the product of the failure of its members to take the practices seriously: the practices of Bible study and prayer and commitment to worship, the failure to see real engagement in Church Meeting as an obligation of church membership. The last serious URC theological conference of which I'm aware, a

gathering of thinkers from across the breadth of
theological opinion called together at Hothorpe Hall by
David Cornick as part of the Catch the Vision process,
came to this same conclusion. The road to renewal, they
said, was through re-engagement with scripture and
prayer and learning to speak of our faith to one another.
They used the language of confidence. Too many of our
members lacked the confidence that the Bible was their
book. They hadn't grappled with their doubts and
reservations about prayer and so simply never prayed
except to go through the motions in public worship.
Having left both to the experts for so long, they really
needed to start from the basics. So *Vision4Life* was born,
not a left brain exercise to pump information into people,
but an experiential approach intentionally designed to
enable seeds of confidence to take root and grow.
Vision4Life has the potential to initiate people into the
core practices of Reformed Christian life. I only wish that
we had done a better job of communicating what we
hoped to see happen. In too many places, I fear, the Bible
materials have been used by the people who always go to
Bible study and the prayer materials have had attention
from the people who are already comfortable with prayer.
It's a stubborn barrier to break down. And it will be the
same come the evangelism year when we are invited to
begin telling our stories. Here, supremely, as I've said,
I see the possibility of fostering Christian confidence,
creating a people who know that they know God,
rudimentary and partial as that knowledge may be. So
what exactly do we do with stories like the ones I told?
First, we take them seriously. Some of them will be self-
centred and some will be trivial. I don't think that means
that God can't be in them. In our immaturity we *are* self-
centred and it takes a long time to develop the ability to
distinguish what's trivial. If that's what God has to work
with, that's what God uses. God cannot speak beyond our
ability to hear, and practice is the only way to learn. I find
myself wanting to deconstruct all the stories as a
scientist would. Surely that young woman cannot believe
that God would influence the weather patterns so as to
engineer a double rainbow in the sky just to save her. It's

not about the rainbow, it's about her readiness to see, and Buechner's too with that license plate that said TRUST. If it hadn't been a rainbow, it would have been a blade of grass poking through the concrete or a bird alighting on a nearby car and looking at her. If it hadn't been a license plate that said TRUST it would have been the understanding smile of a stranger or a shaft of light breaking through the clouds or whatever. We are meaning-making animals. It is what we do. That is how God speaks to us and it is only faith that recognises the voice as God's. If psychology wants to call it the superego or whatever, that will all be very interesting. It would certainly explain the voices in Barbara Brown Taylor's head. I would love to know how it works, not least because my story is almost identical to hers. And let's be clear that no scientific explanation will make God obsolete. It will only reveal how an Other other God engages with us crumbs who otherwise would have no capacity for discerning this loving mystery at all. We take people seriously and we listen to them. We listen especially to the people we find ourselves wanting to disregard. It is the flaw in our precious tradition, that it is the product of such a narrow collection of minds and experiences. Scripture has been a hindrance as much as a blessing in shaping our attitudes towards women and children and foreigners and slaves, let alone anybody who engages in a same-sex relationship. We listen in deeper ways because we are conscious that there are many voices we have failed to hear in the past. It is when we have listened and those who tell their stories feel heard that we have the opportunity to teach. The minister who is the trained theologian will have a particular role to play here, but the congregation of amateur theologians may also have an impact. The teaching needs to be ever so gentle to start. I remember teaching an elders training course once. One lovely man, sincere, dedicated, thrilled and humbled to have been elected an elder, told us that the reason he was a Christian was that his life had been spared in the war when so many of his friends had been killed. He reckoned God had a purpose for his life. Somebody challenged him – does that mean God had no purpose for the lives of the people who died? That did it. He resigned from the eldership and would never let anybody persuade him into any kind of leadership ever again. We all know what it's like to have our feelings hurt. We need to remember that novice theologians are vulnerable to having their thinkings hurt. Everybody has to start somewhere. And then through good teaching we grow and mature until we can be teachers ourselves. I believe that we'd be hard pressed to find a URC member anywhere who doesn't have a story like the ones I've told buried somewhere inside. These are the raw materials, I believe, for the beginnings of serious spiritual and theological exploration. They are where our reasoned discourse connects with people's questions, where doctrine becomes personal. I don't know any secrets for eliciting the stories other than patient and attentive pastoral care that expects such stories to be there. But for many of us confidence begins with the

> I believe that we'd be hard pressed to find a URC member anywhere who doesn't have as story like the ones I've told buried somewhere inside.

affirmation of that connection, that the rainbow or the license plate in our history is akin to the burning bush or the encounter with Cornelius, and that therefore this tradition of ours isn't remote and the province only of experts, but our rightful home too, where we live, where we can claim our place.

With the confidence that comes of finding ourselves at home within the tradition comes also the ability to share the faith with somebody else. I can't see any other way that the folk in our pews are ever going to be evangelists. But if as crumbs on the paper bag who have caught a glimpse of glory, and have had their glimpses affirmed, and have been given a language to talk about it, they encounter other crumbs with other glimpses, which is what the people around us are, all of them, then just maybe a conversation can begin. It will be what our culture regards as authentic, not because of its scholarly footnotes, but because of the voice of personal experience. Christian confidence, then, comes from the connection between our personal experience of the reality beyond our senses and our inheritance in scripture and tradition. I submit that it is a prerequisite for any serious renewal of our churches as lively centres for theological enquiry. Our stories, mature and immature, are the raw materials for the theologies by which we will make sense of things individually. And they are the indispensable training ground for a people who together seek to be guided by the Spirit of a living God. If we learn to claim them and share them, then just maybe we will have the makings of a people who can look you in the eye and say, 'My faith in God is the most important thing in my life.'

References

1   James Alison, *Broken Hearts & New Creations: Intimations of a Great Reversal*, London: Darton Longman & Todd, 2010. p. 103.

2   Ibid., p 104.

3   Frederick Buechner, *Telling Secrets*, San Francisco: HarperSanFrancisco, 1991, pp. 49-50.

4   Barbara Brown Taylor, *An Altar in the World*, Norwich: Canterbury Press, 2009, pp. 109-10.

RENEWING REFORMED THEOLOGY
Marginal Voices, Diversity and Renewal: Reforming God-Talk

Michael Jagessar

"How can the presence of BAME members and other marginal constituencies' shift/influence/fire-up conversations about reforming theology?"

Marginal Voices, Diversity and Renewal: Reforming God-Talk

Michael Jagessar

Stirring the imagination

A caption in a recent issue of *The Baptist Times* (September 3, 2010) carried the comment by Richard Rohr: "Reform the Church, don't leave it". A question may be: how much is the church open and willing to change and be renewed to create constructive spaces for the reform to take shape? What would be the reformers take on and response to this caption?

This summer, our family holidays took us through the Cevennes (France) and included a visit to the Musee de Dessert, an excellent site that documents the history of French Protestantism and especially the persecution of the Huguenots. One could sense from the thoughtful displays and collection, the deadly marginalisation of voices different from that of the dominant religious view of the day. We were struck by the extent to which the marginalised Protestants decided to live and practice their faith, by meeting in inaccessible places and behind bolted doors to read/proclaim the word and celebrate the sacraments, in spite of the persecution, execution, imprisonment and enslavement/banishment on the galleys of French warships.

A few images on display capture this: an artist impression of a preacher and a gathered community high in the mountains; a pastor standing in a "Hulk-like position" between his anxious congregation and approaching soldiers; baptism around a fireplace in a home with a member of the family firmly holding on to the bolt of a bolted door; a mirror behind which the Protestant Bible was hidden; a collapsible pulpit and an area dedicated to all those who fled to Amsterdam, London, the Americas, Caribbean and South Africa. Are there insights from the God-talk and faith-acts of these faithful that can help our conversations on renewing reformed theology today in the United Reformed Church?

Trying to imagine some of our newer migrant churches/Christians of the URC along the line of the fleeing Huguenots and them being asked (if they are remembered) to make a presentation at significant gatherings of the United Reformed Church – where, how and when will they appear on the programme or in the shaping of the programme offer interesting and connecting insights with marginal and dissenting voices across history and contexts. I am always curious about the location of marginal or diversity content presentations at conferences. Like jesters at the dining table-table of the elected, we often stand entertainingly and 'signifyingly' out of place!

> Are there insights from the God-talk and faith-acts of these faithful that can help our conversations on renewing reformed theology today in the United Reformed Church?

There is some assurance that it was late in the night and high in the mountains of the Cevennes, curious Nicodemus and the French Protestants did manage to usurp the canon of rigid/restrictive orthodoxy, albeit at a cost.

This conference hopes to contribute to deepening the intellectual life of the United Reformed Church by: encouraging intellectual seriousness and relevance to the life of congregations in the United Reformed Church. From my perspective (Black and Asian Minority Ethnic [BAME] and postcolonial) "intellectual seriousness" is a very loaded and suspect phrase. Is the implication that theological discourse has died in the URC because it is not carried out in a certain way, from a certain place and by a certain group of voices? Who or what determines "intellectual seriousness" in the United Reformed Church? God-talk has been happening in spite of the fact that the voices may not be the expected ones! This is certainly so among the BAME constituencies I am working with – in and outside of the church. How can "intellectual seriousness" avoid becoming another way of drawing a line or prescribing theological discourse in the United Reformed Church? How can the ethos of "*semper reformanda*" challenge and release "intellectual seriousness"? In encouraging intellectual seriousness how do **WE** reconfigure the "we" of the urc, giving agency to the local, diversity and difference and the relevance of reformed God-talk for today? What does 'intellectual or theological seriousness' have to do with the fact that our church-life is in a sorry shape, characterized by shrinkage, lack of orientation and theological confusion? [cf Welker 1999:136-152]. I raise these questions because the reality as Shirley C. Guthrie once observed is that "the greatest barrier to faithful proclamation of the good news – and the greatest barrier to others' hearing and believing it – is the self-righteous exclusiveness of insiders" [Campbell 2000: p.6], especially those of us who think of ourselves as progressives. We are all guilty – however open we may be!

Renewing reformed theology is timely as it is a challenging undertaking. As I reflected on the theme, a number of other questions arose: what does it matter theologically to us that Reformed theology is retrieved, celebrated and renewed? Would it make us a better, more faithful, relevant and exciting church? Might there be something particular within the reformed ethos that we can draw on for cutting edge mission and ministry today? Can we carry out this exercise without addressing the harms of enlightenment hegemony of which the Reformed heritage has been a significant player? How does the enjoyment of God (drawing on a reformed idea – Westminster Catechism) more powerfully enter our God-talk, language and practices to create spaces for human flourishing that resists the dehumanizing logic of the restrictive economics that presently rule our lives? How might such joyous desire for a generous God enable us to respond to the contemporary challenges of newer migrants, refugees and those seeking sanctuary at our gate – all of which concern theologically the subject matter of boundaries and marginality?

Intercultural journey

At its 2005 General Assembly, the URC officially declared itself a multicultural Church and pledged commitment to empowering the whole church towards just, inclusive and transforming mission and ministry. The URC's history of being an inclusive church that gives agency to BAME Ministries, however, has a long and varying history, from the Church's inception in 1972 (and before that). This declaration was only a first step towards an inter-cultural ethos, which includes the need to address organisation/polity, narratives, worship, ministry and theology. We are presently pushing the conversations on an intercultural church with a broader and more inclusive understanding of culture that challenges all of us to move out of our comfort zones. As a church our *uniting, reforming, non-conforming* and *marginal* characteristics, our own struggles with the issue of identity or identities, and our changing and complex landscape have combined to create an intercultural adventure that offers fascinating vistas to any renewing agenda.

Notwithstanding, in terms of our gathering I wonder how many of us here have read the writings and engage with BAME theologians of the URC and other ecclesial traditions in Britain. And what difference is it making to our God-talk? What is the connection between our declaration of intent (a new confession if you may – meaning that theology is happening), the reality that 10% of our membership (including children and young people) and many of our growing congregations come from the BAME constituencies, and renewing reformed theology? How does the intercultural vision challenge (is challenged by) and add to (and receive from) the reforming tradition/ethos and renewal of the United Reformed Church? How can the presence of BAME members and other marginal constituencies' shift/influence/fire-up conversations about re*form*ing theology?

I suspect that one can reasonably argue that "marginality" has been a key factor in much renewal of theology and of the church throughout its history. Dissent rarely comes from the centre. This pattern is still evident in the renewal of the contemporary church. One can therefore reasonably deduce that marginal or subaltern communities within the United Reformed Church have the potential to do just that. The United Reformed Church started out, if you wish, as a fresh expression in its own time, with a sense of movement/moving bringing together inherited reformed features of various textures to its ethos. This movement has unfortunately evolved into a heavily weighted structure. Recent efforts at rethinking our calling are geared at regaining this sense of movement and freshness. I must concede that the way we govern and order our life may be too difficult to change. What I am confident about, however, is that we

> We are presently pushing the conversations on an intercultural church with a broader and more inclusive understanding of culture that challenges all of us to move out of our comfort zones.

can create, release and nurture spaces where subversion and daring on the edge projects can happen, that is funding fresh departures within the family. Renewal (*renovare* – to again make anew) will only happen on the edges where such spaces are released and encouraged.

I am working with the understanding that theology (God-talk) is always a work of faith inseparable from the lived experiences of the everyday life and ought to point towards liberating transformation. The emphasis on existential realities and primacy of praxis over theory is reflected in the writings of all BAME liberation theologians in Britain. For us, God-Talk" is laced with multiple meanings. It can mean that *God talks* or that we can *dare to talk about* God, even *discern the tongue of*

God or that God-talk is inseparable from *human-talk*. The most humbling implication, however, is the provisional and tentative nature of our God-talk, lest one misrepresents the Divine. While reformed theology may not have given enough agency to experience, its own layered narratives reflect contexts and experiences, with all its complexities. The strength of the reformers has been that their God-talk reflected the authentic ring of their lived realities and the complex nature of their own needed internal conversations – no wonder the idea of *semper reformanda*! This, I perceive as a cue/key for the renewing of God talk in the reformed contexts of the URC and this is a contribution all marginal voices – starting with their experiences – can bring to the table.

> The strength of the reformers has been that their God-talk reflected the authentic ring of their lived realities and the complex nature of their own needed internal conversations...

Towards an intercultural way of living

Diversity ought not to be a novel idea within the reformed family and especially the United Reformed Church. We, walkers of the Jesus Way, embody diversity with our mixed ecclesial and cultural heritages. Reformed theology has never been monolithic, even though within its theological discourse there are distinctive trajectories and contributions. [McKim 2001: xiii]. As the late Lukas Vischer observed:

"Although the Reformation sprang from the same basic impetus everywhere, it took a different course in each place, according to local conditions and historical factors. Not only did the confessions being formulated accent differing points, but there also emerged varying models of the church...Each of these models builds on a different *experience* in relation to state and society." For the Reformers these varying accents were perceived positively, so long as "the gospel is preached and the sacraments administered according to the institution of Christ" [Willis & Welker 1999: 266]

Alan Sell reiterates this point and further notes that the "diversity within the family is not only doctrinal, ecclesiological, liturgical and historical". It is "linguistic and cultural" as well. He goes on to note that it is unwise for any part the family to "imperialistically impose its socio-theological stances upon another." In his view, "[t]he future vitality of Reformed theology depends on its willingness to engage contemporary views and its openness to a consideration of theological insights from today's differing voices," [Willis & Welker 1999:436]. For the historical reality is that "the tradition has been enriched by its varieties and diversities of expression" [McKim 2001:xiii] within the distinctiveness of the reformed tradition vis a vis other ecclesial tradition. Hendrik Vroom offers some helpful imageries in this regard:

> "If we learn to see the tradition like a river going through different landscapes and trying to find its way through hills and fields, we have to accept that the tradition allows for some differences. The Reformation had several sources and also now shows different streams going in different directions. At present more members of WARC member churches live in a non-Western than in a Western context and the Reformed tradition is in a process of exchange with other cultures as well." [WARC 2008:202]

Something must be said about tradition, as the appeal for renewal often ends up re-inscribing "dead faith" (traditionalism). Just recently, my PA placed a clipping from the *Church Times* on my desk about the future of the Church (Church of England) and its missionary calling, arguing that the Church in repentance needs to recover *"true mission"*. The author's idea of true is actually locked into a fossilised view – very much *untrue* of the complex historical realities of the period he was referring to. Tradition is a dynamic process – always in formation. But as Brian Gerrish has rightly observed:

"There will always be a sharp difference between those who understand faithfulness to tradition as the *preservation* of past doctrines and those who understand it as the recognition that past doctrines may be worthy of *development*." [2003:5] Tradition (and theology), like our understanding of the church is *reformata et semper reformanda*, Tradition is traditioning as reformed is reforming! Renewing reformed theology must include a critical scrutiny of the past (traditions). This is the most challenging undertaking for all of us (including the BAME constituencies). "Criticisms of the past," writes Talal Asad, "are morally relevant only when the past still informs the present – when contemporaries invoke the authority of founding ancestors against each other. In criticizing the dead, one is therefore questioning what they have authorized in the living." [1996:328] When texts of the past (our tradition) still continue to hegemonically form and inform contemporary ecclesial life without being aware of the outmoded world and structures from where these have come from to form the basis for our theology and practices, it is high time for critical reflections. Renewing reformed theology necessitates a critical interrogation of all we have inherited! Here is a timely reminder from the late Edward Said:

> "Appeals to the past are among the commonest strategies in interpretations of the present. What animates such appeals is not only disagreement about what happened in the past and what the past was, but uncertainty about whether the past really is past, over and concluded, or whether it continues, albeit in different forms, perhaps." [1993:1]

The reformed tradition itself yields resources that question and challenge its own development, and which interrogate as well as complexify and complement predominant and popular (in different senses) themes within itself. Tradition is therefore rightly described as 'living' in that it is to some extent flexible and so capable of its own redefinition and transformation. It is thereby also always to some extent provisional, being populated with counter-voices and contradictoriness. Such a view is crucial, I think, if appeal to tradition is not to become a tool to enforce uniformity and the subjugation of minorities to majorities.

Reformed theology is not only diverse: it is also and always "unfinished business"? [McKim 2001: xv] Hence, the imperative to continue to listen to God's word in Scripture and be open to the leading of the Holy Spirit" so that "new insights can emerge" [McKim 2001: xv]. For us the past is indeed always prologue – a costly and challenging vocation. This understanding and belief of the early reformers – the discovery of evangelical freedom – created a renewing and transforming storm not only in church but across whole societies. [cf Welker 1999: 152] Thus, it seems to me, the question of renewal of reformed theology cannot be merely an exercise in identifying and listing beliefs that are at the heart of reformed theology. Renewal has to do with priorities for our God talk and its consequences for faith and faithfulness today. One of the priorities is that of grace to recognise that in God's abundance we embody diversity and difference and we need each other for renewal, as much as we need the movement of the Holy Spirit.

> Renewing reformed theology necessitates a critical interrogation of all we have inherited!

This is the vision of the inter-cultural journey. The intercultural vocation calls us to move beyond a mere recognition of the presence of a multiplicity of cultures/diversity with little or no interaction beyond one's own group, as this only offers a diminished sense of our common vocation together around the table of Christ. The invitation/ journey is towards deeper, active and critical interactions and mutually reciprocal relationships among and between diverse groups (entering the threshold of the other). Such a process involves a movement beyond a dialogical relationship towards transformation in all parts of the life of Church. It is an invitation for *all of us* to journey beyond our cultural/theological comfort zones and boundaries to discover new insights of the Divine and what it means to be followers of the Jesus Way *together*, while allowing for multiplicity in that vision of *togetherness*. And this journey – a gift of grace – means that together we enable each other to participate and experience inclusion by creating a culture of inclusion: characterised by "mutual inconvenience" (embracing each other's differences); courageously imagining new ways of being Church so that the variety of 'giftings' are shared and received in ways that delight, enrich, renew and transform congregational lives. The intercultural journey offers exciting vistas for renewing reformed theology!

> ...this journey — a gift of grace — means that together we enable each other to participate and experience inclusion by creating a culture of inclusion...

Some postcolonial questions
I appreciate the insights of Brian Gerrish as I sense these counter attempts to restrict the reformed tradition to a checklist of tenets and dogmas. He speaks of "the Reformed habit of mind" characterised by at least five marks: 1) *deferential*: a habit of critical deference to our forbearers (not hagiography) with commitment and openness; 2) *critical* – critical reflection on past and present alike for the sake of a more authentic and confident witness of the church; 3) *open* – to wisdom and truth wherever they are to be found – in the unlikely places of places; 4) *practical* – a commitment to both edification and transformation of lives and society; 5) *evangelical* – that is the habit of continually bringing theological reflection back to the gospel". [Willis & Welker 1999:8] Gerrish's framework offers both permission for continuing dialogue and hope for constructive critical engagement in any project of renewing reformed theology. In the spirit of the five marks, allow me to raise some questions from a

postcolonial perspective. A stumbling block to renewal on our diverse landscape (cultures & faiths) may be the inability to see the connections between our inherited reformed doctrines/traditions and empire/imperial practices.

One of the shortcomings of our multicultural discourse is with *culture* – that is the tendency to read culture (in multi/inter-cultural) as having to do only with the ethnic other rather than recognising that we are all cultural and complex beings and that within each group there are further cultural diversity. The early reformers were very much living is diverse cultural and imperial contexts and it is interesting to read about their own wrestlings with identities, differences, political alliances and ways in which they had to negotiate these and have also excluded others who did not think like them. Renewing reformed theology, in its backward glance to our reformed heritages, is also about an intercultural engagement – hybridity – not about returning to some notion of pure reformed doctrines – as there is no such thing! Relationships of dominant and dominated, marginalised and oppressed become complexly locked into an inter-weaving journey.

It is not insignificant that the appeal to a transcendent sovereign God has been employed (and still deployed) in support of the dynamics of empire. History is replete with examples (distant and not so distant) of the powerful controlling the weak by giving an unhealthy agency to God's transcendence, omnipotence, judgement and command as means of fostering passivity, fear and a 'pie in the sky' faith. Further, the way we have constructed and articulated God's sovereignty had imperial implications for Christology: that is the Lordship of Christ to the exclusion of servanting (mutuality). Our confessions, hymns, preaching and prayers are replete with this: "the Christ who reigns in power and who is Lord over all life and all nations"! [Campbell 1992:431]. Such theological notions imbibed over years of conditioning continue to play a role in enslaving, marginalising and shutting down diverse and transgressive God-talk/conversations. A question we need to pursue in our renewal quest is where and how reformed theology has played a central role in the culture of empire by creating and legitimising colonialist forms (inhospitable/restrictive/arrogant) of knowledge. Many from the BAME constituencies come from 'former' colonies and have embraced and even internalised much of the 'worst of theological notion'. I am raising these questions not to lay moral blame but as a genuine attempt to help us rediscover "the theological surpluses" that are not value free but are ours to participate in and share. This was what John de Gruchy had in mind when he observed that "Reformed theology needs to be liberated from various captivities" [1999:106]. He argued a case for the critical "retrieval of reformed symbols of faith", those geared towards the cause of social justice. [Willis & Welker 1999:109]

At the heart of our reformed/reforming ethos is the place of Scripture and our dependence on the promptings of the Holy Spirit [see *The Manual* of the URC]. Reformed, word of God and Holy Spirit are inseparable ideas. Whatever our confessional statements-acts of confessing, it is "always referenced to the textuality of the Word of God in Scripture" [Moltman in Willis & Welker 1999:125]. "Reformed theological reflection" writes Cynthia Campbell, "is grounded on the witness of scripture. When Reformed folk say that 'theology matters', they mean that the Bible matters – the Bible as story of God and God's people...The Bible is the place Reformed Christians begin and to which we return in the journey of discernment." [Cynthia Campbell 2000: viii]. The Reformation saw a critique of reading the Bible (and it access to the laity) that resulted in some new formulation of the Christian faith. As Cynthia Campbell suggests:

> The alteration of a cultural or ideological framework allowed the truth of the gospel to be heard anew. But all ideology and all cultural contexts are limited and

must constantly be criticized by other voices and experiences. [1992: 430]

The irony is that in spite of our deep respect for the Bible, we have also managed to adopt an uncritical stance in our hermeneutics and history of interpretation. The 'tidalectic' dynamic – the process of ebb and flow (mingling) of interpretation and re-interpretation, has been neglected. A postcolonial perspective will certainly wish to raise questions here; but more than that it would wish to raise fresh questions about the interpretation of texts from the time of the reformers with the view of detecting, questioning, challenging and exposing how the dominated are represented by the dominant, the link between power and knowledge and the locating of ideologies in plots and characterisation in texts and their interpretations. What, for instance, in the arriving at and solidifying of reformed doctrines and confessions, happened to the marginal and dissenting voices within the Reformed family? How have these been represented? What is the link between the deposit of reformed faith/confessions, empire, the missionary enterprise, mission and theology?

...he railed continually against the duplicitous and immoral behaviour of the British government which had not hesitated to use the opium trade as a method of wresting territorial and commercial advantage from the Chinese.

Another point of critical engagement that marginal voices from a postcolonial perspective will wish to raise is the traditional reformed emphasis on revelation and how we articulate God's self-disclosure. [cf. Campbell 1992:426] The view that God-talk (theology) is a reflection in the first instance on and interpreted by Scripture and not reflection on human experience is problematic for marginalised groups. The irony is that God's call is not propositional. It is experiential. This point is related to my query about "intellectual seriousness" and the tendency to perceive the primacy of "experience" as a suspect way of doing theology. As some scholars have noted, the suspicion is related to the concern that BAME, liberation, feminist, and postcolonial perspectives have "removed the 'sovereignty' of God and located God entirely in the realm of human experience" – which in my view is not true. It is only that these perspectives attempt at having more honest God-talk [Campbell in McKim 1992: 427]. If at the heart of traditional reformed theology God stands transcendently alone, then it will follow that we would find it difficult to represent or re-image the Divine as vulnerable, in solidarity with our deepest anguishes and humans as co-creators with God. For Cynthia Campbell a closer scrutiny will reveal the shortcoming of this position. She notes: "

> "there is an intrinsic and necessary relation between the medium and the message. To suggest that theological truth can be separated from the people and circumstances in which revelation took place is, among other things, to deny the significance that the incarnation occurred in one very specific place, culture, and time and not any other. [McKim 1992:428]

One of the characteristics of BAME congregations is the deep sense of a calling to live joyful and generous lives. It is especially reflected in their worship and attitude to life. The spiritual energy, hospitality, and passion for mission that is found among these URC congregations here at home and among our partner churches in African Asia, Pacific, and the Americas/Caribbean is often a wake-up call from our frozen faith and ecclesial life. It is interesting that for all the reformed family's ponderousness and seriousness, to the first question in the Westminster Shorter Catechism – *what is the chief end of human beings?* – the answer given is, *to glorify God and enjoy [God] forever*, highlighting enjoyment.

Enjoyment is linked to generosity as we claim belief in a God of abundance. Often, however, longer established Christian communities operate on the principle of scarcity. What the postcolonial method does is point us back to the places/points in history where we have inherited and developed our restrictive habits: showing how biblical writers, interpreters and theologians from the time of the early Christian community have attempted to restrict hospitality only to those who are in line with the author/interpreter/group approved theological position. Often theological rhetoric is misused and hospitality manipulated in order to bring those who are thinking differently in line. Renewal will never happen if scarcity is the orienting metaphor of our life together. It is not insignificant that one of the most meaningful images of human salvation is the banquet table where God in Christ in the generous host (and meal). Salvation is imaged as a carnival where people will come from all directions to share in the feast. Thus, in rethinking what it means to be an intercultural community, the imageries of table, feasting and banquet have become prominent in racial justice and multicultural ministry conversations. Our inhospitality will not go down lightly in the eyes of the Divine, not even our attempts to hide behind warnings of God's inhospitality according to some narrow readings of biblical texts. We believe in a generous God of radical hospitality. Living this belief offers renewal that will touch our souls, energise our emotions, renew our worship and prayer life, and send us out with a new, exciting and transforming song of faith and faithfulness on our lips and hearts. That is theology in action – not from a desk!

Going out with joy
"The future," observes Robert Bohl, "does not belong to a church that is dishonest". We are dishonest when we refuse to recognise and honour our intra-diversity and enjoy the surpluses of our heritage; when with designed unawareness we cannot see and welcome "the other" of our community who are already in our midst; when tradition shackles us to static ways of being; when our liberalism becomes intolerant through our perceived

intolerance of others; when we are unable to engage critically with our inherited doctrines and to learn from each other and when we lose the sense of adventure and openness to the unpredictable movements of the Holy Spirit. A dishonest church lives in fear, is insecure and takes on the burden of conserving 'the faith'", hence restrictive proclivities. The future, on the other hand, as Bohl contends, belongs

> "...to a church that knows what it does not know; to a church that relies upon God's grace and wisdom and has in its weakness and ignorance a radical confidence in God: to a church that is strong in faith, joyous and certain yet self-critical; to a church filled with intellectual desire, spontaneity, animation and fruitfulness; to a church that has the courage of initiative and the courage to take risks; to a church that is completely committed to Jesus Christ. In short, the future belongs to a thoroughly truthful church."
> [2000:72]

Alan Sell has warned us that our "theology needs to be kept in perspective" – meaning that in our renewing project, as we sharpen our pencils, it is imperative that we remember the biblical urging about "letting our light so shine". For, as he writes, "what shall it profit us if we end up with sharpened pencils and dimmed lights"! [Sell in Willis & Welker 1999: 441] We have a sacred and layered story that has been hijacked from us, and it may be that in our time the culprit is passing as orthodoxy itself.

References

Talal Asad, "A Comment on Translation, Critique and Subversion," in
Between Languages and Cultures: Translation and Cross-cultural Texts,
A. Dingwaney and C. Maier, eds. (Delhi: Oxford University Press, 1996),
pp.325-332

Robert Bohl, "The Church that is alive is loyal to the past but open to the
Future" in *Renewing the Vision* (2000, p.66-73)

Cynthia M Campbell (editor), *Renewing the Vision: Reformed Faith in the
21st Century* (Geneva Press: Louisville, Kentucky, 2000)

Cynthia M. Campbell, "Feminist Theologies and the Reformed Tradition" in
Major Themes in the Reformed Tradition edited by McKim (1992: pp.426-
432)

B.A. Gerrish (editor), *Reformed Theology for the Third Christian Millennium*.
The 2001 Sprunt Lectures (WJK Press: Louisville, 2003)

Brian Gerrish, "Tradition in the Modern World: The Reformed Habit of the
Mind." In Willis and Welker, *Toward the Future of Reformed Theology:
Tasks, Topics & Traditions* (Wm.B Eerdmans Publishing Company: Grand
Rapids & Cambridge, 1999) [pp.3-20]

John de Gruchy, "Toward a Reformed Theology of Liberation: A Retrieval of
Reformed Symbols in the Struggle for Justice." [Willis & Welker 1999:
pp.103-109]

Donald K. McKim, *Introducing the Reformed Faith: Biblical Revelation,
Christian Tradition, Contemporary Significance* (WJK Press: Louisville,
2001)

Donald K. McKim ed, *Major Themes in the Reformed Tradition* (Wm. B.
Eerdmans: Grand Rapids, Michigan, 1992)

Elna Mouton, "Surprised by New Contexts: Challenges of Reformed
Exegesis from within Liminal Spaces" [pp.230-241] in Alston & Welker
2007.

KwokPui-lan, Don H. Compier & Joerg Rieger eds., *Empire: The Christian
Tradition: New Readings of Classical Theologians* (Minneapolis: Fortress
Press, 2007)

Alasdair MacIntyre, *After Virtue: A Study in Moral Theory* (Notre Dame:
University of Notre Dame, 1984).

Edward Said, *Culture and Imperialism* (Chatto & Windus: London, 1993).

Alan P.F. Sell, "The Reformed Family Today: Some Theological Reflections"
in Willis & Welker 1999: 433-441]

Michael Welker, "Travail and Mission: Theology Reformed according to
God's Word at the Beginning of the Third Millennium" in Willis & Welker
1999: 136-152]

Lukas Vischer, "The Church – Mother of the Believers", Willis & Welker
    1999:262-282.

Hendrik M. Vroom, "On Reformed Identity" in *Reformed World* (58/4
    December 2008) pp.189-206

David Willis & Michael Welker, *Toward the Future of Reformed Theology:
    Tasks, Topics & Traditions* (Wm.B Eerdmans Publishing Company: Grand
    Rapids & Cambridge, 1999)

Wallace M. Alston Jr., Michael Welker (editors), *Reformed Theology: Identity
    and Ecumenicity II: Biblical Interpretation in the Reformed Tradition*
    (Wm.B Eerdmans Publishing Company: Grand Rapids, Michigan &
    Cambridge: UK, 2007

A UNITED REFORMED CHURCH PUBLICATION

RENEWING REFORMED THEOLOGY
Renewing the United Reformed Church
John Bradbury

"By far the most exciting and
theologically engaged set of debates
I have ever witnessed on the floor of
general assembly concerned the
revised statement of faith in
inclusive language'

Renewing the United Reformed Church

John Bradbury

In 1552 John Calvin famously responded warmly to Archbishop Thomas Cranmer's suggestion of a general meeting of Europe's Protestants. ' ...the churches are so divided, that human fellowship is scarcely now in any repute amongst us, far less that Christian intercourse which all make a profession of, but few sincerely practise...Thus is it that the members of the Church being severed, the body lies bleeding. So much does this concern me, that, if I could be of any service, I would not grudge to cross even ten seas, if need be, on account of it.'[1] It never happened because Edward VI was dead within a year and Cranmer speeding his way to a martyr's death. Nine years later Calvin mooted the idea to Matthew Parker, Elizabeth's Archbishop. He expressed interest, but nothing happened.

At this stage in proceedings, starting a paper by saying that I'm not sure there is such a thing as 'Reformed Theology' might sound rather strange. But I'm not quite convinced there is. The Reformation in general did not take issue with any of the major creedal confessional statements. The Nicene and Chalcedonian Christological statements are never challenged, neither are the Trinitarian formulations. Calvin's first edition of his institutes is a commentary on the Apostle's creed, and Schleiermacher uses this theological reality of the acceptance of the early confessional statements to call for a completion of the reformation by reforming just such notions[1]. Theology, *per se* was not the issue of the Reformation – or at least not in its foundational doctrinal sense. I have heard papers about Reformed theology that purport to lay out our foundational aspects – it turns out we are Trinitarian, we value scripture pre-eminently, we hold to a doctrine of election (however understood), the church is vital as are the sacraments ... and there is normally not much that any good Catholic, Anglican or Orthodox theologian would not say. Maybe the emphasis and tone are different, but in substance, to be Reformed is to be an Orthodox Catholic Christian. In a huge number of respects, Calvin and Aquinas are really rather close in their concerns. Both are primarily commentators on scripture, both even have rather a high doctrine of election (which one can't really escape if one reads scripture) and so on.

So what is it, then, to be Reformed? More specifically, to be the United Reformed Church? This paper is setting out not specifically to answer that question, or do anything much sensible at all. In fact, to any students of mine sitting there, this is an object lesson in how not to be an academic. I'm going to make sweeping assertions, unfounded statements, and tackle far, far too much in a tiny amount of time. Do as I say, not as I do. However, at this point in a conference like this, it strikes me that it is a moment to broaden our scope, to stimulate the ideas, thinking and doing of theology and church that must go on after this conference as we reflect on the whole experience and all of the papers, and if Martin's vision for what this is about, actually means anything. It is a paper that will probably upset everyone somewhere, and is offered more in the way of an Aunt Sally to knock down, than anything else.

> ...(this) is a paper that will probably upset everyone somewhere, and is offered more in the way of an Aunt Sally to knock down, than anything else.

I do think there are certain emphases in the Reformed tradition – kinds of family resemblances within Reformed churches, that do mark us out theologically. The absolutely centrality of the word 'grace' standing in the midst of that. Nothing but nothing happens but for the grace of God – most centrally our creation, redemption and consummation. But we can't claim exclusive concentration on that theme – for that would simply be untrue. Scripture plays a foundational role too, though that must never be read as if the witness of the church throughout the ages to the reception of that scripture is not deeply significant – Calvin's engagement with the 'Father's' of the Church being central and foundational to him. Scripture, however, for Calvin always has the last word, though we are warned that we must take very seriously the words of those who have read, engaged with and ordered their lives around that scripture who have gone before us. Scripture, though, is central to other traditions too. I think where perhaps we begin to be distinctive is in two specific areas that I want to dwell on briefly. Firstly, the Reformed tendency to perpetually re-state the faith, and secondly, our approach to the embodiment of our faith in the life of the Church. I want to take these two ideas, explore where they come from briefly, explore the challenges and opportunities of the context we find ourselves in presently, and suggest various ways forward for the United Reformed Church, drawing on those things that are distinctively Reformed – which are in reality about the particular way we embody and live the gospel faith.

One of the most interesting reflections on the perpetual need for the reformation of the Church comes from perhaps a rather unlikely source: that of Rowan Williams, in his theological postscript to his book on Arius. To shorten and simplify it massively, he argues that in the great debate between Arius and Athanasius, Arius wished to uphold the unity of God the Father as sole originator of all creation (the son essentially becoming the first creature through whom the Father creates) and was actually upholding some very traditional theological and scriptural language. What Williams argues is that Athanasius and the Church as it ultimately follows him, realises that sometimes you have to say the new thing to continue to be in continuity with the original, apostolic gospel. Simply keep saying the same thing over and over again, and in the end you are no longer saying it as the world, language and culture move on around you. To allow God ultimately to be defined by Christ, rather than defining what Christ must be by received formulations concerning God, was in fact that radical position. Thus to continue upholding the scriptural understanding of the incarnation, new, and in fact non-scriptural, language had to be employed. Working out how to say the old thing in the face of the language and needs of the present is in fact the task of theology. That is why it is so vital – and I fear we are not always very good at it. The question of theology, as Williams sees it in the light of this historic debate with Arius, is "What, in our own terms, is it that is distinctive in the Christian proclamation, and so in the Christian form of life?'[2]

The Reformed tradition, whilst not being able to claim this theological understanding or process as its own (and this is now a fairly obvious point having cited a rather Catholic kind of Anglican to get us into this thought), has always and instinctively understood the need to be doing just this. We read and read again our scriptures, and we listen with seriousness to the voices of those who have read our scriptures before us, and we make sense of that here and now, in the present, and find ways of articulating our faith for the here and now. We see this is the huge proliferation of Reformed Confessional statements at the time of the Reformation and up to our present day. There are hundreds of the things, often from tiny Reformed churches representing areas no larger than we would think of as a modest sized town at the time of the Reformation, or the most unlikely events precipitating new statements of faith, like the socialist revolution in Cuba causing the Cuban Reformed to try and state it again in the way called to by those events. Frequently such statements are prefaced by the request that we are open to revising them (as in the preface to the Second Helvetic Confession) if through engagement with scripture, better ways can be found to state the faith. We see this in the URC itself, and it was a new statement of faith that brought the church into being (the Basis of

Union basically being such a statement). By far the most exciting and theologically engaged set of debates I have ever witnessed on the floor of general assembly concerned the revised statement of faith in inclusive language – where it felt like the Church was doing extraordinary soul-searching about who and what we were – we were being formed in our identity in those debates. Ultimately, the resultant statement is very rarely ever used, as one of our oddities is that we write these things endlessly, but don't actually ever use them much in worship or even catechesis – such as we engage in it. It is intrinsic to us, however, that we continual to grapple and do not expect the formulations of our faith from previous generations to suffice for today – even where we still take those formulations very seriously indeed.

There are, however, various dangers in this. I'll point to just a couple. On the one side, there is the inherent danger of a kind of unbiblical doctrinalism in this reformed approach. It presupposes that scripture 'contains' doctrine, which we can then state in propositional truth claims, a rather emotive way of talking of confessions of faith. This, it seems to me, is the meeting of the felt need to confess, with the love affair of modernity with just such propositional truth claims and results in a certain form of doctrinalism that ends up feeling very unlike the multi-layered and complex texts of scripture which are history, story, poetry, law, letter, apocalyptic, parable, gospel and so on. Finding the language to tell our story today which enables us to bring scripture into the midst of our life in the world is one thing, turning scripture into a set of propositional truth claims one can sign up to or not is quite another. The other danger comes from a slightly different direction, which is that it ultimately wants to apologise scripture away – and yes, I am kind of

> Finding the language to tell our story today which enables us to bring scripture into the midst of our life in the world is one thing, turning scripture into a set of propositional truth claims one can sign up to or not is quite another.

playing on the word apologise here. The resurrection, miracles, Noah's flood, the seven day creation are not read theologically as the word of God, but strangely literally (for those who actually tend to want to fight off so-called literalism). With such a literal reading, they are then seen as 'un-true'-, and explained away, often with the help of pop-psychology. Hence, the gospel is apparently separated, as in Bultmann, from the 'myth' in which it is written leaving us with actually what amounts to a different sort of propositional truth claims, this time nearly always more about psychological or sociological states of being – or Bultmann's 'authentic existence' and the like. Both of these approaches are, to my mind, both dangerous and absolutely not what was in Calvin's mind as he set out to help people make sense of their faith and life in the world and offer a reading of scripture to do so (which is his intent in the *Institutes*), or that stating of the faith today which is re-formulated because to say the same thing is actually no longer to say the same thing at all.

> The resurrection, miracles, Noah's flood, the seven day creation are not read theologically as the word of God, but strangely literally (for those who actually tend to want to fight off so-called literalism).

This need to make sense of our faith, and speak of it today – which is a call precisely to do theology, is absolutely vital. We are all too often forced into responding to critics like Dawkins by either saying we don't need to believe the seven day creation anyway, or by finding ways of making the unbelievable believable. Rarely does one hear of someone responding in the terms of our Christian faith, talking positively about what it is that our scriptural account of creation is positively speaking of and the things which really matter within it – which have absolutely nothing to do with whether Dawkins is right about evolutionary biology or not. I suspect I'm preaching to the converted here, though.

So...stating our faith, and doing theology are part of our essential being. It is a very Reformed resource we have to draw on. The other I want to briefly examine is the way we go about becoming Church, and about how we order ourselves. What is fascinating is that there is no particular 'set' Reformed order or polity. We are generally 'concilar' – though some of us have bishops too. We don't have a received three-fold order of ministry, but rather what we have varies. In the URC we have ordained Elders and Ministers of Word and Sacrament and CRCWs. Other places have ordained teachers too, or ordained deacons. We tend to meet in council, but at what levels and layers of the Church's life rather depends on where one is. This is actually related to the previous point. Lutheranism has one defined confessional statement – the Augsburg confession, and a much more closely defined church order. We have many such statements and have many forms of order too. Calvin is clear that Church government must be that which is expedient for the time and place, and is not permanently dictated. What is of the essence of the Church is that the Word is proclaimed and the sacraments celebrated. What is nearly as important, and at times makes it into the marks of the church, is that the church is ordered. Order matters. Vitally – it is how we ensure that the Word is indeed proclaimed and the sacraments celebrated. What that order is, however, is not fixed. Whilst I'm still unconvinced that the URC got its restructuring right a few years ago when Districts disappeared (not that I was a great supporter of them, by the way), I am delighted that I belong to a church than is capable of such a radical restructuring as we undertook. We might, perhaps, have gone yet more radical still...

What I want to say is that between this necessity for perpetually re-stating our faith through continually grappling with scripture, and our flexibility in how we go about being church, lies two of our great riches which can help us as we move into the future. Two things, however, that one might at times think hang rather tentatively by a thread.

We must acknowledge at this point, that we are living in an exceedingly difficult moment to be engaging with our faith and what it is to be church. I've been fascinated to spend some time recently looking at the debates between sociologists as to where we are in European terms regarding religious belief and practice. There are those like Steve Bruce who argue strongly that 'secularization' is almost complete. Churches are dead and dying, as is belief in God. He argues that those who deny this, do so out of their own personal convictions on the matter. On the other hand are those like Grace Davie, who argue that religion is far from dead, and that people still believe, but they do not belong anymore. Much touting of data is used, but what struck me was some of the questions used in gathering the data. Just taking the European Values survey for a moment, we can see just what kind of statements people are being asked to identify themselves with. Which of these, I wonder, do you all identify with? "There is a personal God", "There is some God, Spirit or life force", "I don't know if there is a God, Spirit or life force", or "There is no God, Spirit or life force". I'm really not quite sure I'd know what to say. Is the God of Abraham, Isaac and Jacob, as made known to us in the person of Jesus Christ a 'personal God' – I'm really not quite sure. Yes...a God who has a personal relationship with creation in the form of a person – but personal in the sense of my personal trainer, personal loan, personal opinion, or my personal shopper...well, not quite. This question is so far from asking about what might be considered a theologically orthodox statement about God, Father, Son and Spirit, that it tells us nothing about the state of the Christian faith at all, I hazard. Other questions asked in such survey's are about 'life after death', 'heaven and hell', and other such 'traditional beliefs'. That there is generally speaking a hanging left over from medieval artistic depictions of such things within the popular imagination comes as no great surprise, but it is a far, far, distance from what we think we are doing when we confess faith in one God, Father, Son and Holy Spirit, revealed to us in the person of Jesus Christ, who is opened to us as we grapple with the aid of the Holy Spirit with the texts of scripture, who we worship and adore, and which provides us with the story by which we make sense of life in the world and find ways, together, of living that life and offers the vision of bodily resurrection and the redemption of all things.

That to get results about religious belief, researchers have to ask questions which concern matters so far from orthodox expressions of the Christian faith, suggests to me that the situation is far, far worse than many commentators dare actually postulate. I think those of us who have worked on the edges of the life of the church and engaged those who have had literally nothing to do with it (rather than those who have dropped off the edge at some point) realise that. The very basic stories of our faith are not known.

> There are still significant numbers of folk out there with some latent attachment to church and faith — but far, far more with none whatsoever.

Possibly my most amazing experience as a minister yet was one Good Friday when a lad in his late teens who'd started coming along to a Friday evening group I baked bread with in Liverpool, asked me what on earth we remembered on Good Friday. He'd never heard of the crucifixion – did not really know what one was. We sat and just read the story from one of the gospel accounts – and it was extraordinary and illuminating to do so with someone hearing it for the first time. But I think that actually a huge proportion of the population are now relatively like that teenager – so much so that to get any results at all the researchers have to ask ever more vague questions. Talking explicitly with younger working members of my congregation about the folk they worked with, they shared my sense that what we might call religious questions were just not on the agenda at all. There are still significant numbers of folk out there with some latent attachment to church and faith – but far, far more with none whatsoever.

I find the language of the French sociologist Daniele Hervieu-Leger helpful, who speaks of there having been a break in the chain of memory within European religion. This, helpfully I think, begins to get to heart of the crisis that we face. Our faith is one in which memory is central. The canon of scripture functions as the authorised memory of our faith, that as it is read and re-read creates the memory of our faith and its identity. The major practices that stand at the heart of our practice of church life, the proclamation of the Word and the sacraments are all pre-eminently moments of the forming of the collective memory of the Church. Christ calls us literally to 'do this in remembrance of me' – and most people now do not, and it is perhaps no surprise that the faith has been almost entirely forgotten in our society – save for a few pop-religious ideas, practices and images. My concern, however, is that this seems worryingly to be affecting the church itself.

If I am hit on the head and suffer from amnesia, and no longer know my name, or where I come from, or my background or history, and those people with whom I am in relationship, then I no longer have any sense of my identity.

In the 'year of the bible' those of us whose ministry is based here at Westminster went out and about quite a bit engaging with some of the material with groups up and down the country. It was fascinating in that initial opening section of the preparatory material when people were asked to name the passages of scripture most significant to them, that the impression we ended up with is that the canon of scripture for the URC seems to consist primarily of the parables of the prodigal son and the good Samaritan! Wonderful parables...but there is a little more to our scriptures than that! Memory is absolutely key to our identity. If I am hit on the head and suffer from amnesia, and no longer know my name, or where I come from, or my background or history, and those people with whom I am in relationship, then I no longer have any sense of my identity. Those who have lived and cared for sufferers of dementia in one form or another know the agony of this well – the person is simultaneously exactly who they always were, but at the same time are no longer them at all somehow. It is a tragic condition. My fear is that there is a considerable danger of the church at the moment suffering collective 'amnesia' – we seem to have forgotten exactly who we are and why we are.

As a former secretary of a pastoral committee I got to do endless vacancy visits and the like to the seemingly endless churches without ministers of Word and Sacrament of the former Liverpool district. There are some wonderful and faithful folk around – and some churches that seem to have rediscovered their sense of identity and their reason for being (some because they do not have ordained ministry of Word and Sacrament, interestingly...) but there are many others for whom if one pushes just a little the sole reason for existing is to keep existing. Mission is not about the extension of the Kingdom, about helping people respond in the here and now to the fullness of life that Christ offers, or to transform the world – but rather because if we don't do something there won't be enough people to do the jobs to stay open. I have heard that time, and time again...too many of our churches really have reached that point where, through sheer exhaustion and overwork, as the same group of people have done the work for often now 40 or 50 years, they have entirely forgotten why they might have started doing the work themselves. And these are folk who often have a deep personal faith that one comes to know and be humbled by when one has spent enough time drinking pastoral cups of tea with them in their own homes – but it is as though they are now on automatic pilot in church life. We need to grasp the nettle in many, many places. Having, in very distressing circumstance, to help a church to do that at one point, one of the members (and almost all joined other local churches and strengthened them enormously) said a few months later to those of us involved at the time that we 'had cut an albatross from around their necks that they had not realised was hanging there'. Where churches are suffering from advanced amnesia (which I maintain is very different from faithlessness) cutting that albatross needs to happen – and we need to address our polity so that those who are least able to take the necessary decisions do not have to take them. To close seems all too often like failure – not maybe the dusk of a Holy Saturday that might well lead to resurrection on Easter morning. At times, folk really do need to have that done for them by the wider church.

We also need to take much more seriously – though here I think I can honestly say continue to take very seriously, how we go about refocusing our collective memory, and reengage our identity as the church. It is hugely heartening that we decided to refocus our life by examining the bible, prayer and evangelism. Fantastic! But we need more, and more and more resources of this sort to help struggling congregations re-find their memories of the faith. I remember presenting the bible year material to a group of lay preachers in one Synod and the excitement there was, and then the bemusement from a few of those present that there was only 4 of these kinds of bible study in the book...not one for every Sunday through the 'bible year'. Heaven only knows whether we could ever produce that high quality of material for churches to engage with every Sunday (or even, actually, whether that would simply stamp on the wonderful creativity of our lay preachers and ministers!) but it was a slightly sobering response.

And in this search for the memory of the church, we need desperately to get the whole church engaging in that quest for finding the words today in which we express our most ancient faith. The whole church needs to be confident in talking about God – which is ultimately what theology is. The sadness is that we tend to be very bad about talking about God within the life of the Church – we'll talk about almost anything else. Until we can do that, mission will be almost entirely impossible!

All of this to my mind can only really begin in one place – our worship in the local church. The chief end of human beings is to glorify God, and that is the primary end of the Church – and that starts and ends in our worship, and draws into it the whole of life which lies between that start and that end. Do we normally expect, never mind enable, our ministers to spend a majority of their time preparing for the proclamation of the Word and the celebration of the sacraments which is their primary and fundamental call? Do we really expect the very best in worship because it is what we are offering to God? Do we expect worship to be the place where the texts of scripture meet with the text of our life in the world in such a way that we begin to see through the divine lens we are offered and make sense of life in our often seemingly senseless world? Do we demand the best quality music, or whatever sort or variety, because we recognise with the Psalmists that this is vital to our praise of God? Vital too, in our communication in a world where music literally provides the mood accompaniment to our lives. Do we expect the best possible crafted liturgy and prayers – and give our lay preachers, ministers and all those who lead worship the best possible resources to help them in that? The recent lay preachers events here at Westminster where we had about 140 lay preachers in three groups through the place in a week reminded me so powerfully that these are some of the most engaged, thoughtful and amazing people in our church life. Interestingly, working with them on the topic of the Eucharist, as they are increasingly presiding at the Eucharist regularly, I discovered that well over half of them are normally engaging in the ministry of Word and Sacrament. I do wonder whether our church order really needs to catch up with our practice and recognise this – are these not

> Do we normally expect, never mind enable, our ministers to spend a majority of their time preparing for the proclamation of the Word and the celebration of the sacraments which is their primary and fundamental call?

really our non-stipendiary ministers, given that non-stipendiary ministry did not turn out as the visionaries who instigated it for the church hoped? Could we have our own form of locally ordained ministry of Word and Sacrament – and then recognise our ministers of Word and Sacrament as also being those who share in a ministry of leadership and oversight which is peculiar and distinctive to them? Our flexible polity would allow this – would that be a sensible recognition of reality?

Do we expect the best possible crafted liturgy and prayers — and give our lay preachers, ministers and all those who lead worship the best possible resources to help them in that?

And I hope you can begin to see how the two things that I've identified that might be particularly reformed – the perpetual recognition of the need to state the faith again for today, and our flexibility of church structures and government begin to come together. How do we unite these two things in serious, sustained and practical practices of church life that will enable us to find the way to re-tell our story in ways in which it can be heard for the very first time by many of those around us?

So...here, in short, are 10 reasonably random ideas to get us thinking:

ONE

Continue the journey of re-engaging with our scriptures. This must pervade our worship and the whole of church life. We must move well beyond those endless debates about physical or bodily resurrection...do those with heated opinions on both sides just not get the fact that neither the words bodily resuscitation or spiritual presence would do...so we get the new word resurrection? Get over it folks. Similarly with the Virgin birth – which speaks so powerfully to us of the reality that in Christ we do indeed see truly God – stopping us inventing God's of our own. It's a theology lesson, not a biology lesson.

TWO

Plough a significant amount of our resources into those things that energise and feed our worshipping life. We presently don't even have a national committee that deals with worship – which is just slightly alarming for a church! Resources, experiences, continuing education, support in music and the visual arts, support for the best possible homiletic practice – these should be at the top of our national and synodical agendas. If not, are we really the Body of Christ any more? We need everything from wonderful prayers and images to employ, to help working out how on earth to deal with the reality that the organist stopped actually being able to enhance worship 25 years ago and at the age of 95 needs to be persuaded to give way!

THREE

Shut lots of churches. Where that memory has been lost, and churches have become albatrosses around the necks of the faithful and survival is now the name of the game, not the worship of the living God and the following of Christ – let us free good folk up to re-find their faith without the massive effort for survival. Otherwise, too many of our churches will cease being churches altogether, and become rather old-fashioned social clubs left over from the 19th century reality of the beginnings of leisure time, without any money to buy it in. Too many already are.

FOUR

Encourage theology at every level of the life of the Church. I'm deeply proud that the URC takes ministerial education more seriously than any other British denomination expecting most of our folk to prepare for four years and supporting us through excellent EM2 and 3 and sabbatical programs. As many of those as possible should go on to engage with theology at the most advanced and stretching level they can, being given extra time to do it whenever they can benefit from it. We need those people who can engage at the highest level with the telling of our story of faith in this sceptical world, in engaging our scriptures, and our practices of church life at depth, at understanding the story of where we have come from so we might see where we are going. This is just vital. As is engaging theology at the local level. Are we adequately dealing with the questions of speaking of God in our worship and local church life. Who was this Jesus person really anyway? Why do bad things happen to good people? Is that Dawkins chap right, after all? The simplest questions are the easiest to ask – yet I fear we're not often very good at giving the space to ask the questions, or listen to those outside the church who are asking them, and giving them the respect of thoughtful and considered responses. We simply must – or we are not proclaiming our faith any more.

FIVE

We must get our act together in terms of polity. To do that, we need to give up some of our cherished regionalisms. Is it really sensible that we now have to find 13 different ways of doing absolutely everything? I wonder how many full time years worth of time we dedicated to coming up with the 13 different structures that now make up our 13 different synods? It took over my life for a while and that of many other folk. How many full time equivalent years of ministerial and lay work have we taken up coming up with 13 different policies on how we deal with lay presidency? Do we actually need 13 different trusts with accompanying officers, legal advisers and the like. We are not a big church that needs breaking into smaller sections to manage ourselves as once we conceived ourselves. Lets sort that out even more radically than we have – rather than pulling more and more full time staff into managing 13 different synod operations as we do at the moment. We are a small church sort of in three nations (the sort of being our strange different ways of being or not being devolved, not our ecclesial status) – let us act as one. Let us do nationally those things that can simply be far more effective in terms of time and cost – and free more local structures to concern themselves with supporting the worshipping, theological and missional life of the church.

SIX

Let us not forget that we are a **United** Church. Being ecumenical and broad is difficult and emotionally draining at times. We feel this most in certain key areas of our life – the most pressing one of recent years being our debates around human sexuality. Those debates themselves revealing just how bad we are at theology, as we bandy bits of scripture around at one another, and rant on about human rights – not a particularly biblical notion. God is more concerned with gracious gifts, not rights. This is perhaps our biggest test facing us at the moment. As we push to be a church that offers a radical welcome – let us never forget that the welcome is God's. We are the unlikely ones who have been engrafted onto the vine of Israel. We are the unlikely ones whom God has included – out of that, we make known God's radical welcome of us that is extended to others. It is never our welcome to give. We do not have the power to include – God includes. We are the included. Let us stop thinking we might be the Father in the story of the prodigal son, and start to realise we are the prodigal son himself. We are the ones welcomed back. And let us live out that call to be the body of Christ. Paul writes to those wretched Corinthians as the Church – he does not threaten to de-church them. Rather he loves them despite everything – and calls them to love one another despite the appalling way they've carried on with one another. As a gay man in the URC I get deeply alarmed when I hear people talking about my 'side', and the fact that we must 'win'. I have deeply cherished theological convictions about the nature and extent of grace, about the nature of our human sin that Christ redeems, about the fact that our Christian identity begins by being baptised and is found in our part in the body of Christ which overcomes all biological or cultural distinctions.

> God is more concerned with gracious gifts, not rights. This is perhaps our biggest test facing us at the moment.

But recognising the most unlikely reality that I have been included by God – I simply cannot but recognise that God too has done the most unlikely thing of including those people with whom I passionately disagree when it comes to the matter of human sexuality. At the moment we are seeking to live with that tension –thank God we are. I do not want to be part of a church that makes me feel safe as a gay man, by forcing others to leave or essentially de-churching them. That is to seek to limit the grace of God which is the only reason I can stand here as a baptised member of the church today. Let us tread very carefully that as we extend a radical welcome, so we do not land up in the ironic position of making some of the church feel excluded to the point of sadly leaving. Let us remember too that radical welcomes can also be radical exclusions. Anyone who has worked with those who've survived sexual abuse (which will actually be everyone in this room, though you might not realise it) should know that radical inclusion can also make a place radically excluding to others. Being the body of Christ is harder work and more complicated than simply any tag like 'inclusivity' or 'welcome' can ever quite get to.

> I do not want to be part of a church that makes me feel safe as a gay man, by forcing others to leave or essentially de-churching them.

SEVEN

Let us explore radical ways of being the community of the Church. Being church is a massively counter-cultural thing to be. In a time and place where we are taught that we are to be radically individualistic, and define myself over and against others as what my inner-self really is, let us not jump uncritically on that bandwagon. Mission is not about getting people together in groups of people just like them – as some theorists behind certain bits of the emerging church agenda seem to think. It's about the full diversity of life in the world finding its place within the body. Let us seek to be radically diverse communities- a truly multicultural church, not groups of people just like us, in terms of race, class, education, theological style or anything else. Let us explore ways of radically doing community too. Bonhoeffer remarked way back in the 20th century, that religious communities probably would have their radical place to play in the re-emergence of the church. I still think he is right, and am deeply saddened that some of the communities we did have in terms of Ginger Groups, or the community team at Yardley Hastings, seem to have gone – communities of faith that formed for a while, and formed those in them into some of our most creative and inspiring church members and ministers. Let's explore what this being the body of Christ really can mean and experiment with new forms of energising community – something the reformation maybe did not handle as carefully as it might. Maybe there was more to the idea of the religious order than we realised.

EIGHT

Let us begin to take very seriously the ministry of oversight within the life of the Church. Leadership and oversight at regional level proves itself time and time again to be vital – and yet we have very little emotional space for it, never mind in our polity. Let us recognise the vital ministry of our Synod Moderators and Church house staff – and let us acknowledge that it is a ministry for which some are gifted and called – and is sometimes a very different set of gifting and calling that local ministry. Exercised well it can be the most uplifting and freeing of gifts to the Church. Let us acknowledge it far more – and also be rather more transparent about it. The Moderators meeting is one of the most influential in the life of the church yet is not a council of the church or really formally recognised or accountable at all. That is a most unorderly bit of Reformed polity. Equally, there are other powerhouses in the life of the church that need unearthing and holding to visible account too – I think most specifically of Synod Clerks who hold the most extraordinary sway over things, and yet their work often goes entirely unnoticed.

NINE

Let us renew our understanding of vocation and the discernment of call. All too often, it seems to me that our understanding of vocation, particularly to ministry of Word and Sacrament and CRCW ministry, has become discerning some kind of inner Gnostic secret knowledge as to whether someone is 'called' or not. We really need to begin to take Paul a little more seriously as he speaks of the gifts of the Spirit for ministry. Too often, our selection conferences seem far too interested in that mysterious inner call, and not in whether the Spirit has gifted a person for the work the church needs doing. Let us not forget Calvin too – the call is for the church to discern, it cannot pretend to know the inner secret call, only the outer call rooted in some very pragmatic things, like the competencies of character and ability to actually do the job. And whilst we are at it, let us think very seriously about whether our amazing lay preachers are not, after all, ministers of Word and Sacrament.

TEN

Let us not be scared. The institutional Church is dying. All the forecasts are that it might not be around as an institution as I come to need my pension. There is a bridge to be crossed there personally, maybe – but whether with a church house in London, 13 synod offices and a sprinkling of Resource Centres for Learning or not – God's people will exist, and gather and worship. Christ's body will make known Christ's gracious love calling us on to live Kingdom shaped lives and loves. That is exciting and wonderful. We set out in faith on this journey into the unknown, knowing only that within the next 20 years church life will become absolutely unrecognisable. And we will still be called to proclaim the gospel, expound the word, remember Christ in his presence with us in bread and wine, bring people into totally new lives and identities in baptism. It is God's church – and it will not be abandoned – even if we are being led into a desert where we will be reshaped into God's holy people once more, regaining our memories and our divine practices of life in the world. And let us dream our dreams and see our visions of what that might be like. Let us be faithful stewards of what we have received, and not be scared about playing our part of the reformation of what we have received as we travel on into God's future. Reformed and reforming. Seeking to state our faith ever anew, and seeking always to be Church in the order and shape we are called to in the here and now. That way, I believe, lies the discovery again of some of the riches of our tradition that God has given us, as we seek to be God's faithful people in the 21st century, in this little Island of the world.

> Let us be faithful stewards of what we have received, and not be scared about playing our part of the reformation of what we have received as we travel on into God's future.

References

1 Friedrich Schleiermacher, *The Christian Faith*, Edinburgh, T&T Clark, 1999, p. 747ff.

2 Rowan Williams: *Arius*, London, SCM Press, 1987/2001, p. 237-8.